Neil Gaiman
and Philosophy

Popular Culture and Philosophy® Series Editor: George A. Reisch

For full details of all Popular Culture and Philosophy® books, visit www.opencourtbooks.com.

Popular Culture and Philosophy®

Neil Gaiman and Philosophy

Gods Gone Wild!

Edited by
TRACY L. BEALER, RACHEL LURIA,
AND WAYNE YUEN

OPEN COURT
Chicago and LaSalle, Illinois

Volume 66 in the series, Popular Culture and Philosophy®, edited by George A. Reisch

To order books from Open Court, call toll-free 1-800-815-2280, or visit our website at www.opencourtbooks.com.

Open Court Publishing Company is a division of Carus Publishing Company.

Printed and bound in the United States of America.

Library of Congress Cataloging-in-Publication Data

Neil Gaiman and philosophy : gods gone wild! / edited by Tracy L. Bealer, Rachel Luria, and Wayne Yuen.
     p. cm. — (Popular culture and philosophy ; v. 66)
    Includes bibliographical references and index.
    ISBN 978-0-8126-9765-0 (trade paper : alk. paper)
    1. Gaiman, Neil—Criticism and interpretation. 2. Philosophy in literature.
  I. Bealer, Tracy Lyn. II. Luria, Rachel, 1974- III. Yuen, Wayne, 1978-
    PR6057.A319Z77 2012
    823'.914—dc23

                                           2012010964

Contents

Traveling with the Gods

TRACY L. BEALER AND RACHEL LURIA

"It starts with doors." This ominous prophecy from a homeless woman to Richard Mayhew, the reluctant hero of *Neverwhere*, is itself a door into understanding Neil Gaiman's stories.

In Gaiman's re-creation of reality, characters like Richard, Coraline, and Shadow, the ex-con protagonist of *American Gods*, often discover enchanted alternate worlds that bump up against the margins of the mundane, the reasonable, and the rational. Because Gaiman typically introduces his fantastic worlds through the eyes of a character who is, like the reader, seeing them for the first time, part of the pleasure of these stories is the joy of exploration—without leaving the chair or, as Rachel prefers it, bed, the reader embarks on a richly described encounter with an unfamiliar place, making these stories fictive travel literature—topographies of the imaginary where the maps are philosophical rather than geographic.

Tracy's first Gaiman-prompted trip was across the grounds of her college campus to a friend's dorm room. That, you see, was where the Dream King lived. As she devoured the *Sandman* series, she learned that comic books weren't just for boys, and that Neil Gaiman had a way of making the most mythic characters and stories feel like people she knew, and places she felt like she'd been. Gaiman gave her permission to take fantasy seriously, and she's been reading and writing about genre fiction ever since.

Rachel's first encounter with Gaiman was also in college—that time of transition and self-discovery—and was also through his *Sandman* series. The book that haunts her most, however, is his *American Gods*. At once a classic road trip story and an epic adventure, the novel makes her re-examine the American landscape and the landscape of myth and legend. Gaiman provides a new map for once familiar territory.

As with all great travel stories, Gaiman's heroes and his readers must mentally, as well as literally, map the unfamiliar spaces in order to understand the rules that govern them. Though travel literature typically describes a traveler exploring a new culture for pleasure and personal growth, Gaiman's protagonists are often forced, tricked, or seduced into entering unfamiliar landscapes where not just their identity but their very lives are threatened. His characters must map and decode the fantastical worlds in which they find themselves in order to survive.

And in doing so, these characters also re-evaluate their own understanding of themselves and the "real" world to which they return. Whether it's through the underground society Richard Mayhew discovers in *Neverwhere*, the ominous shadow home described in *Coraline*, or a vision of America as a battleground for forgotten gods, the Gaiman reader may finish a book but begins a lifelong journey, discovering the new worlds within their self and, perhaps, hiding just beneath the surface of the ordinary.

Gaiman's fascination with encounters with the unknown is what makes his stories work as travel writing. Though most often associated with descriptions of "sun-drenched beaches" and "quaint bed and breakfasts" that are meant to lure one away from home to "exotic" destinations, this is not the sole nor the true purpose of travel writing. Travel writing is, at its heart, about exploration and discovery, how finding the strange and new invites reflection. It is more about what you come to see inside yourself, how you map those strange and "secret worlds" that are found within, than what you see on the horizon, though this insight can only come through looking out on a new landscape.

Not all who visit unfamiliar places are travelers, some remain only tourists. Tourists remain always at a distance from their experience. Hidden behind the protective wall of camera and guidebook, the tourist remains detached, unchanged by the experience. The tourist believes himself or herself to be the center of the universe, the new location merely a novelty to be toyed with before returning home unaltered. The traveler, on the other hand, engages and is transformed.

The chapters in this book offer a philosophical guidebook for travelers navigating Gaiman's imaginary spaces. Using philosophy as a lens, the authors describe, explore, and engage with the places and people found in Gaiman's short stories, novels, screenplays, and comics, in a sense discovering them anew for fans and casual readers alike.

Gaiman's stories do more than simply confirm the power of travel or the fragility of bounded space. They have the same transformative effect on the readers as they do for the fictional characters who populate them. Travel doesn't always take you somewhere nice and you aren't always transformed for the better for having gone. However, if the journey is made through books, which both immerse you and leave you at a safe remove, you are always improved for having gone.

Gaiman's writing takes his readers through alien space and as is the nature of such writing, transforms the reader. Paul Fussell says "We are all tourists now, and there is no escape," but reading Gaiman shows that this doesn't have to be true. In his Newberry Award acceptance speech, Gaiman writes:

> We who make stories know that we tell lies for a living. But they are good lies that say true things, and we owe it to our readers to build them as best we can. Because somewhere out there is someone who needs that story. Someone who will grow up with a different landscape, who without that story will be a different person. And who with that story may have hope, or wisdom, or kindness, or comfort. And that is why we write.

For anyone who has read Neil Gaiman's stories, we know that he builds them well, and the roads they take us down leave us changed forever. We may have been tourists once, but we are travelers now.

Gods
Behaving
Badly

1

Mr. Wednesday's Game of Chance

ELIZABETH SWANSTROM

"It was crooked," said Shadow. "All of it. None of it was for real. It was just a setup for a massacre."

"Exactly," said Wednesday's voice from the shadows. "It was crooked. But it was the only game in town."

—NEIL GAIMAN, *American Gods*

Meet Mr. Wednesday, the contemporary North-American incarnation of Odin himself, the one-eyed, bloodthirsty Norse god of poetry, wisdom, and prophecy. In *American Gods*, Odin is a ribald old goat with a black Rolex watch and an ax to grind. His beef? His worshippers have been waning, his sacrifices dwindling, and his popularity as a deity yielding to the newer gods of Media, Technology, and Broadcast—not to mention a rag-tag assortment of African, Asian, and Indo-European gods that have come over on various boats, along with the immigrant people who believed in them, throughout American history. Clearly, there's not enough worship to go around, so Wednesday needs to take action.

His plan? By teaming up with his son Loki, and by misleading the other gods into thinking they are enemies, he plans to stir them up to such a frothy outrage that they will fight each other to the death on a battlefield of his choosing. With this plan in place, Mr. Wednesday reckons on causing enough mayhem, enough violence, and enough bloody carnage to revitalize his godhead. And just to make sure there is sufficient chaos and strife, he plans to sweeten the deal with a human sacrifice. The victim? His son Shadow.

The Sucker

Meet Shadow, a modern-day incarnation of the Norse god Balder. We don't know as much about the Norse gods as we do about, say, the gods of ancient Greece, but we do know that Balder, Odin's son, holds a special place in Norse lore. According to Snorri Sturluson's *Prose Edda* (written around A.D. 1220) our richest historical source for the pre-Christian religion of Scandinavia, Balder is "the sweetest-spoken and the most merciful" god in the entire Viking mythos (admittedly, this might not be saying much). Unfortunately for Shadow, Balder is also the most gullible, both in the thirteenth century *Edda* and in Gaiman's twenty-first-century re-telling.

In *American Gods*, Shadow is a muscle-bound convict who likes to do coin tricks. Strong, sweetly naive, and eager to please, he's exactly what you might think a modern-day Balder should be, save for one important detail: he has no idea of his place in the North-American version of the Norse pantheon, nor that such a pantheon even exists outside of books. At the beginning of the novel, Odin's gambit—and Odin himself—could not be further from his mind.

About to be released from prison, Shadow looks forward to reuniting with the love of his life, his wife Laura, who looks equally forward to his release. However, a few days before he's about to be freed, the warden calls him into his office to let him know that his wife has died in a freak car crash. Stunned, Shadow leaves prison and travels to the funeral. These early events seem merely to conform to the capricious random generator that is fate. Tough break. Bad things happen to good people. We know this. Yet it is shortly after, while Shadow is in transit, that these circumstances begin to emit a causal odor.

Shadow's flight keeps getting bumped. He is supposed to fly directly to the funeral home in Eagle Point, but the plane gets re-routed to St. Louis because of bad weather. So he gets put on another flight, runs to make it, only to have it canceled. After running from gate to gate and plane to plane, he begins to feel like "a pea being flicked between three cups, or a card being shuffled through a deck." This is an apt simile, not only because it matches the shuffling momentum Shadow experiences, but also because it foreshadows the revelation that Shadow is, from the very beginning, a hapless component within a larger con. He doesn't know this yet, however, so he makes one last dash across the airport and gets put on a flight that leaves from the same gate he'd just run from. This flight is full, so, in another (seeming) twist of fate, Shadow gets moved to first class. And it is here, on the only empty seat in the entire plane, that he meets Mr. Wednesday, who taps his finger against his black Rolex and mouths the words, "You're late."

Now, what's extraordinary about this chain of events is not that planes get re-routed and flights get canceled. This sort of thing happens with such frequency that a smooth, eventless flight is more of the exception than the rule. What pushes this sequence of events into the philosophically murky territory of causation is the fact that Mr. Wednesday appears to have orchestrated it. Coincidence—the idea that two things can happen simultaneously—is one thing. This is altogether something different. How so? There are at least ten related events that unfold sequentially to create this initial meeting.

1. There is Laura's death, which

2. results in Shadow's early release from prison, which

3. puts him on a certain plane, which

4. gets re-routed, which

5. results in a re-scheduled flight, which

6. is cancelled, which

7. forces him on yet another flight, which

8. is full, which

9. means he must take the only open seat on the plane (in First Class, to boot—how often does *that* happen?), which

10. puts him right next to Wednesday, who offers him a job.

At this initial meeting, Shadow rejects the offer for work and leaves Wednesday behind. Yet like an Ace of Spades in a dirty game of poker—drawn firstly to complete a highly unlikely inside straight (the odds are 253.8 to 1), and then secondly an even more unlikely full house (693.2 to 1), and then thirdly to top off a nigh-impossible royal flush (a whopping 649,739 to 1)—Mr. Wednesday keeps turning up.

Shadow rents a car and, on the (seemingly) chance suggestion of a gas attendant in the town of "Nottamun (pop. 1301)," stops for a bite to eat at "Jack's Crocodile Bar" in the middle of nowhere.[1] And who should be there to greet him? Wednesday, naturally, grinning "like a fox eating shit from a barbed wire fence." And here, again, Mr. Wednesday offers Shadow a job. Tired from Wednesday's relentless haranguing, Shadow— father's son that he is, even though he doesn't know it yet— attempts to con his way out:

> Shadow took a quarter from his pocket, tails up. He flicked it up in the air, knocking against his finger as it left his hand, giving it a wobble as if it were turning, caught it, slapped it down on the back of his hand.
> "Call," he said.
> "Why?" asked Wednesday.
> "I don't want to work for anyone with worse luck than me. Call."
> "Heads," said Mr. Wednesday.
> "Sorry," said Shadow, without even bothering to glance at the quarter. "It was tails. I rigged the toss."
> "Rigged games are the easiest ones to break," said Wednesday, wagging a square finger at Shadow. "Take another look at it."
> Shadow glanced down at it. The head was face-up.
> "I must have fumbled the toss," he said, puzzled.
> "You do yourself a disservice," said Wednesday, and he grinned. "I'm just a lucky, lucky guy." (p. 34)

Wednesday's clearly up to something here. Shadow knows it, we as readers sense it, and Wednesday's shit-eating grin confirms it. Yet Shadow gets suckered, all the same. But how? While another, less causally savvy god might simply have plucked Shadow from jail and made him get to work through

---

[1] The name Nottamun also appears in an English folk song from the Middle Ages, "Nottamun Town":

In Nottamun Town, not a soul to be seen.
Not a soul would look up, not a soul would look down.
Not a soul would look up, not a soul would look down
To show me the way to fair Nottamun Town. (*Roud Folksong Index*)

the sheer force of his divine will, Wednesday's *modus operandi* is more subtle and smooth, and therefore more effective: he stacks the deck unfairly and deals it against his mark. Faced with such power, Shadow does what many a mortal would do when put in a similar situation: he succumbs. Shadow agrees to work as Odin's henchman, even sealing the deal with three sips of mead.

But Shadow is unaware of his role in Wednesday's greater scheme, or, indeed, that Wednesday *has* a greater scheme, and it is not until the climactic final moments of *American Gods*— as Shadow hangs from a Virginian version of the mighty Yggdrasil, the tree of knowledge that connects the nine worlds in Scandinavian mythology—that he realizes that he has been a pawn in a confidence scheme of epic proportions, that he has been thoroughly and utterly duped.

For Shadow, this realization is crucial, because it allows him, finally, to participate actively in a game he did not even know he was playing. For the reader interested in philosophy, this realization is equally crucial, because it foregrounds how *American Gods* manages to foil any commonsense understanding of causality.

Hume's Pool Cue

The most common, and common-sense, idea we have about causality is the notion of derivative causality, which we inherited from antiquity. This idea—that every cause has a result, and that, conversely, every event is the result of a cause—is an ancient philosophical premise that dates back to Democritus, to Leucippus, and to Plato, who writes in the *Timaeus* that "everything which becomes must of necessity become owing to some Cause" (section 28A). Yet the notion of derivative causality is most forcefully put forward by the Stoic Philosophers of ancient Rome. It is Seneca the Younger, that most Stoic of them all, who puts it most succinctly:

> It is the connection of cause to cause which out of itself produces anything . . . nothing has happened which was not going to be, and likewise nothing is going to be of which nature does not contain causes working to bring that very thing about. (*On Divination* 1.125–26)

Seneca would know. His knowledge of cause was hardly that of a lofty academic. He got caught in a treacherous and inescapable web of consequence that eventually resulted in his own elaborate and painful suicide, ordered by the mad Emperor Nero.

The idea that everything derives from an identifiable cause, perhaps not surprisingly, sets off a causal chain of its own. When people start believing that everything that happens had to have happened because it was caused, they begin to doubt that there is such a thing as chance, or such a thing as free will. And this is a threat to traditional religion.

The concept of derivative causality shifts and re-settles during the Middle Ages and the Renaissance, but it experiences its most dramatic upheaval in the eighteenth century, with the Scottish philosopher David Hume. A child prodigy, Hume enters the University of Edinburgh at age twelve, ostensibly to study law, but instead becomes obsessed with the philosophy of antiquity and the issue of causality particularly. Hume's idea of causation is clearly informed by the ancient writing of the Stoics, as well as by the more nuanced understanding of derivation and responsibility that Aristotle articulates, and the theory of flux and flow that the pre-Socratic philosopher Heraclitus outlines. Yet Hume's novel take on causality distinguishes him from any prior philosopher.

Hume's notion is that causality is not, in fact, a physical law that can be proved by experiment. All that we observe is that some things happen together, and if they always happen together, we start to expect one event to occur after the other event. Hume calls this happening together "constant conjunction." Consider, he suggests, a simple game of billiards:

> Here is a billiard ball lying on the table, and another ball moving towards it with rapidity. They strike; and the ball which was formerly at rest now acquires a motion. This is as perfect an instance of the relation of cause and effect as any which we know, either by sensation or reflection. Let us therefore examine it. (Abstract of *A Treatise of Human Nature*)

Hume does just this, and through his examination of these two billiard balls he comes up with three criteria for causation.

The first criterion is the "contiguity of time and place," which means that in order for something to result in something else, the first thing must be in proximity to the second, just as the first billiard ball must be in proximity to the second billiard ball, in order to strike it; secondly, causality requires "priority in time," which means that for something to cause something else to happen, it must precede it in time. So far, this conforms well enough to our common-sense idea of cause and effect. It is Hume's third criterion that shakes things up:

> Let us try any other balls of the same kind in a like situation, and we shall always find that the impulse of the one produces motion in the other. Here, therefore, is a third circumstance, viz., that of a *constant conjunction* betwixt the cause and effect. Every object like the cause produces always some object like the effect.

At first glance, this third criterion seems merely to suggest the repetition of the first two. However, Hume goes onto explain that it is this repetition that *gives rise to* our concept of causality. The causal relation does not emerge from anything inherent in the billiard balls themselves, nor, in fact does *any* causal association result from the objects that seem to cause them: "When I see a billiard ball moving towards another, my mind is immediately carried by habit to the usual effect," Hume says, and insists that "There is nothing in these objects, abstractly considered, and independent of experience, which leads me to form any such conclusion." Hume's point is that we never observe causes and effects. Cause and effect is not something that we see in nature, but something we invent.

Recognizing that we are creatures who tend to associate things in our minds, Hume nails the fact that we become habituated to certain associations, that we learn to accept them as inexorably, causally linked, even though there might not be any necessary relation between them at all. Mr. Wednesday understands the power of association via constant conjunction quite well—so well that he is able to weave a web of causality so dense that its consequences appear to be driven by chance.

The Two-Man Con

As we've seen, the early moments of *American Gods seem* to reveal Odin as a master manipulator of chance. Yet it is precisely the opposite that is true. Odin doesn't manipulate chance. By definition, chance is "the absence of cause," independent of derivative laws, and therefore immune to manipulation, even from a divine agent (unless, of course, that divine agent is Chance itself, as we shall see). Instead, Odin's actions point to a set-up. A good set-up requires that everything be in place from the very beginning, and Odin and Loki construct a very good set-up indeed, a set-up so cleverly fore-grounded that it can only be seen in retrospect.

To see how it works, we have to go back in time, before the death of Shadow's wife, before his time in prison, before the death of his mother, who refuses to reveal the name of his father, and all the way back before Shadow was born, even. It all begins here, with the seduction of Shadow's mom by a smooth-talking, one-eyed con man under the romantic, prismatic light of a dance hall's disco ball, thirty-three years before the novel begins, on the very night of his conception. Nine months later, a sucker is born.

Loki and Odin need Shadow to get the battle going. But they have to figure out how to motivate him without letting him know that he's their sacrificial lamb or calling attention to their larger scam. Wednesday even spells it out for him, later on:

> "I needed *you*. Yes. My own boy. I knew that you had been conceived, but your mother left the country. It took us so long to find you. And when we did find you, you were in prison. We needed to find out what made you tick. What buttons we could press to make you move. Who you were." (p. 534)

Enter Low Key Lyesmith, a "grifter from Minnesota" who shares Shadow's prison cell. Loki gets himself planted in the slammer with Shadow so he can identify Shadow's weak spot, which turns out to be how much he loves his wife Laura. With this information in hand, Loki leaves so he and Wednesday can refine their plan. By killing Shadow's wife, they think they will make Shadow their man. It almost works.

But how so? How are they able to pull off a scheme of such epic proportions, with such a simple plan, which is basically nothing but a two-man con: "Two men, who appear to be on opposite sides, playing the same game" (p. 532). The answer is misdirection, or the art of distraction. In terms of Hume's notion of constant conjunction, misdirection takes advantage of the way we form causal connections. Because we make causal inferences based upon associations, misdirection nudges us to form causal links where none exist and, even more disastrously for Shadow and his wife, to ignore the links that actually do.

It's Called Misdirection

Misdirection is named at least twice in the book, first, in an innocent offhand comment made by Shadow, and secondly, by a sinister Odin who reveals he's been the one doing the misdirecting all along. In the first instance, early on, Shadow's perfecting a coin flip, and Wednesday compliments him on his skill:

> "I'm just learning," said Shadow. "I can do a lot of the technical stuff. The hardest part is making people look at the wrong hand."
> "Is that so?"
> "Yes," said Shadow. "It's called misdirection." (p. 104)

The second time it happens, near the end, Odin is still confident that his scheme is unfolding as planned. He's so confident, in fact, that he attempts to praise Shadow for the role that he's played: "You did everything you were intended to do, and more. You took everybody's attention, so they never looked at the hand with the coin in it. It's called misdirection. . . . To tell the truth, I'm proud of you" (p. 530).

Misdirection takes advantage of the mind's tendency to ascribe causal relations from instances of constant conjunction, but it only works if it is subtly employed, and it takes Shadow the bulk of the novel to hone in on how it's happened. The instances of misdirection or distraction are almost too numerous to count, but there are a few key moments worth noting.

Firstly, early in the book, during that fateful evening at Jack's Crocodile Bar, a very drunk Mad Sweeny, a seven-foot tall leprechaun who loves Southern Comfort, warns Shadow explicitly about Mr. Wednesday. As Wednesday explains to Shadow what his job will be, assuring him that he will be well paid and well cared for, Mad Sweeney butts in:

> "He's hustling you," said Mad Sweeney, rubbing his bristly ginger beard. "He's a hustler."

"Damn straight I'm a hustler," said Wednesday. "That why I need someone to look out for my best interests." (p. 37)

In this classic moment of misdirection, Wednesday, by agreeing to the general truth of Sweeney's statement, distracts Shadow from the more specific claim. He *is* being hustled, individually, at this very moment, but because Wednesday admits to general knavery, the other part slides by, even though Shadow's instincts have already flared up, prompting him to call Wednesday a liar, right to his face. But Wednesday doesn't blink. Instead, he says, "Of course. And a good one. The best you will ever meet" (p. 32). Again, admitting the truth about his general nature obscures the specific treachery, managing to assuage Shadow's instincts, which are, in fact, dead on the money. Wednesday *is* a good liar—the best—and he is at this very moment lying to Shadow about the full scope of his job description.

Another instance, very subtly deployed, comes at the very beginning of the novel. Lowkey has lent Shadow a copy of Herodotus's *Histories*, a book chock full of outrageous whoppers and historical curiosities. Yet Shadow hones in on one particular tale that Herodotus tells, the story of Croesus. The reference is fleeting, but it speaks volumes about the causal web that Loki and Odin—and, even more impressively, Gaiman—are weaving:

In his travels to the east, the great Athenian statesman Solon visits the richest man in the world, Croesus, who asks Solon who he thinks is the world's most fortunate man. Solon answers with examples of several common men Croesus has never heard of, and Croesus, who has spent a lot of time and energy to impress Solon with his riches, grows tired of fishing for compliments and finally asks him the question, point blank: "My Athenian guest, do you so much despise our happiness that you do not even make us worth as much as common men?" Solon's answer is just as direct.

I set the limit of a man's life at seventy years; these seventy years have twenty-five thousand, two hundred days. . . . Out of all these days in the seventy years, all twenty-six thousand, two hundred and fifty of them, not one brings anything at all like another. So, Croesus, man is entirely chance. To me you seem to be very rich and to be king of many people, but I cannot answer your question before I learn that you ended your life well. (*Histories*, 1.32.1)

Solon's answer affirms the power of chance and suggests that man cannot know what fate has in store for him. Hence, although Croesus now seems wealthy and fortunate, he still has many days left in which things might go awry. Simply put, the story of Croesus expresses a familiar refrain: "It's not over until it's over."

By introducing Shadow to this story, it seems that Lowkey Lyesmith is looking out for Shadow, by tuning him in to the vagaries of fate. And so he is. But by calling attention to the seeming capricious whims of destiny, he also obscures the fact that he, Loki Lie-smith, is a prime architect of Shadow's misery. The seeming interest he takes in him distracts Shadow from his devious machinations and allows his meticulously plotted scheme to unfold.

The insertion of Herodotus here, early on, is a fiendishly clever move on Gaiman's part, because it makes a sucker of Shadow and the reader both. Both, unless they have Wednesday's powers of foresight and causal prowess, will have not seen it for what it is, a classic case of misdirection. The book is filled with such moments. And they are so successful because, unlike red herrings, which lead down entirely different pathways, instances of misdirection are so close to the truth that they don't raise any red flags.

Constant Conjunction

We're trained to think of the relation between cause and effect as a given pre-condition for living, not a flexible, deviously woven fabric, subject to manipulation. Our common sense notion of causality is this: Something happens—let's call it x—which results in something else happening—let's call it y. These two events can be put into a symbolic relation that can be written like so: $x \rightarrow y$. If, for example, I roll a six-sided die (again, we can call this event x), my roll will yield one of six results, with equal probability (and again, we can call this y, the consequence of x). A simple case of $x \rightarrow y$? Not so fast.

What constant conjunction shows us is that even this straightforward example, which suggests a simple causal relation between action and result, falls apart fairly quickly. My roll of the die is dependent upon several things, including the mechanism of the die, my decision to roll it, toss it, or kiss it ("for luck"), as well as the sensations I experience when I do so. The principle of constant conjunction forces us to acknowledge that causality is a link that *we* make, that what we *perceive* as causality, even if it appears to demonstrate proximity and priority, again and again, is dependent upon the mind that experiences it. What appears to have a clear cause, in other words, may well be the result of something else entirely.

My example of the die, for instance, becomes even more complicated when we think about my personal history (perhaps I am a habitual gambler, but not a very good one, and my hand shakes in nervous desperation as I bet the family farm), about what circumstances have brought me to make the roll in the first place (perhaps I am like Loki, an out-and-out thief, who laments the loss of his former glory and is looking for revenge: "You take all the belief and become bigger, cooler, more than human. . . . And then one day they forget about you, and they don't believe in you . . . and the next thing you know you're running a three-card monte game on the corner of Broadway and Forty-third"), as well as what sorts of events and objects have facilitated the creation of the die in the first place (perhaps it is oddly weighted; or it has an extra six on one of its sides; or perhaps the kiss I have given it for "luck" has disguised a steamy breath that will make the side I blew on stick to the table. Any one of these possibilities would emerge from a nexus of naughty objects and sneaky intentions, and would give me an unfair advantage).

What Hume's notion of constant conjunction shows us, in effect, is that what seems to be a simple, two-part formulation $(x \rightarrow y)$ becomes dizzying in its complexity and shakes the foundation of causal certainty with any measure of scrutiny. Does Hume, then, suggest that the universe is lawless, random, and governed entirely by chance? Nope. Not by a long shot. What Hume does say that probability exists, and is measurable, but that what we perceive as causation comes from human experience.[2]

---

[2] Hume is a compatibilist. Compatibilism is the theory that free will and determinism can both be true: there is no contradiction between them.

Yet at the same time, an awareness of constant conjunction allows us to step back and look with fresh eyes at any situation, in order to sift true cause from mere correlation, and sniff out a set-up from the distracting mist of coincidence. In this way constant conjunction offers an antidote to what Odin and Shadow both refer to as "misdirection." We can question the original association, re-think the links of consequence, zoom out, and see a whole host of causal possibilities. And this is just what Shadow does.

The Sucker Vanishes

When the epiphany finally hits—revealed to Shadow as he hangs from the mighty Yggdrasil, guarded by three bored Norns, while the sharp-toothed squirrel Ratatosk scurries to and fro—it does so with a sharp wallop of clarity: "Shadow saw it then. He saw it all, stark in its simplicity. He shook his head, then he began to chuckle . . . and then the chuckle became a full-throated laugh" (p. 514). Shadow realizes in this instant that Wednesday's large-scale scam is entirely consistent with the smaller-scale games of chance—coin flips, stacked cards, and loaded dice, not to mention a dazzling variety of confidence schemes—that have peppered his encounters with Wednesday as a whole.

But how does the realization that he's been duped help poor Balder, tied to a tree? Doesn't it simply confirm Odin's mastery of misdirection, and, hence causality? Up to this point in the novel, yes. If the novel were to end here, it would certainly be a useless epiphany. But remember the lesson of Solon and Croesus? It's not over till it's over. At this point, it's definitely not over. In fact, although he doesn't know it, Shadow has been preparing for these final moments—the end game—from the very beginning.

If Mr. Wednesday is a master of causality, Shadow is a student of chance, and sometimes the talented student can surprise and surpass his teacher. In nearly every scene in the novel, we see Shadow practicing sleights of hand. Flipping coins is how he keeps himself occupied in prison, with a book of coin tricks and time to kill. And unlike Odin, he uses his skills to help people, teaching coin tricks to small children, entertaining adolescents, and helping out friends on the road. And when he's finally released, while waiting for Wednesday to recruit him for work on the coming war, he decides to pass the time in training, to "practice his coin sleights and palms until he was smooth as anything" (p. 256). He masters The Miser's Dream, the Classic Palm, Coins Through the Table, a Pointless Coin Trick (of his own invention), and the Sucker Vanish.

Given Balder's gullible nature, The Sucker Vanish is a particularly apt trick for him to master. Indeed, it's one of the most popular coin sleights of all time. J. B. Bobo, the author of *Modern Coin Magic*, writes of it that "No better effect than this could be used to close a routine of coin tricks. It is a dandy for the wiseacre and perfect for the kids" (p. 50). The Sucker Vanish is also a suitable title for the final revelation that marks the novel's close. When Shadow finally realizes he's been the sucker of Wednesday's scheme all along, as he's hanging on a tree and floating in and out of death, he knows what to do. With help from Easter and an ancient Thunderbird (avian, not automotive), he leaves the tree, seeks out Wednesday, and confronts him: "I'm tired of being played for a sucker. . . . Just show yourself. Let me see you" (p. 532).

In this moment he calls out Odin and Loki and pulls the rug out from their larger scheme: that Shadow will be sacrificed, a bloody battle will be waged, Loki will dedicate the battle to Odin, and Odin will return from the dead one hundred times more potent than before. And this is how it would have turned out, if not for an earlier toss of a golden coin that sparked an entirely different causal chain, one that ends up putting the kibosh on the line of dominos that Odin means to set in motion.

Who Loves the Sun?

At the beginning of the novel, in the unlikely venue of Jack's Crocodile Bar, Mad Sweeney slips a coin in the jukebox, and the box begins to play a song from the 1970s, "Who Loves the Sun?" by the Velvet Underground:

> Shadow thought it a strange song to find on a jukebox. It seemed very unlikely. But then, this whole evening had become increasingly unlikely. (p. 39)

As unlikely as the song seems to Shadow, however, "Who Loves the Sun?" is a wholly appropriate theme song for a seven-foot tall leprechaun who waxes poetic about his gold, the "sun's treasure . . . there in those moments when the world makes a rainbow . . . in the moment of eclipse and the moment of the storm" (p. 228).

In this same scene, Sweeney does a coin trick that leaves Shadow stymied, because it looks for all the world that instead of relying on sleight-of-hand to produce the gold coins that shine in his palm, he has "plucked them out of the air" (p. 40). Shadow demands to know how it's done, but Sweeney's reply is maddening: "It's the simplest trick in the world. I'll fight you for it" (p. 41). They fight; Shadow wins the fight, and with it wins a piece of the leprechaun's gold.

Most of us are familiar with clichés about leprechauns—their pots of gold, their wish-granting capabilities, their four-leaf clovers, and, if the commercials that surround Saturday morning cartoons are to be believed, their insatiable appetite for a certain breakfast cereal. As unfortunate as these depictions of the "little people" may be, in terms of raw luck—both good and bad—Mad Sweeney fits the bill.

When he plucks the gold from the magic hoard and gives it to Shadow, Mad Sweeney throws a wild card into Odin's masterful plan and, in larger philosophical terms, introduces an element of chance into an overall causal universe. This action sets off an entirely different chain of events, one that Wednesday has not at all predicted. The coin, a souvenir from the hoard at the rainbow's end in Celtic lore, has the power to raise the dead. And this is exactly what it does. Unaware of its magical properties, Shadow drops the coin in his wife's open grave. The result of this action is that Laura returns to life and makes it her mission to protect her husband from Wednesday's wiles and to redeem herself for her own wandering ways.

Luck Be a Lady . . .

Laura, however, does not enjoy a *complete* resurrection. She's more like a zombie, really, and when she makes her first post-mortem appearance shortly after her burial, she does so as a shambling corpse in Shadow's hotel room. Understandably, he's a bit rattled by this, so she leaves him alone, retreating to the shadows of the novel's sub-plot. She does not, however, abandon him. Instead, she shadows his journey every step of the way, striving to find out what's going on, and updating him intermittently, even as her flesh continues to decompose.

Laura sniffs out the scam right before Shadow does and, as Shadow hangs from the tree, his life draining away, Laura hunts down Loki, disguised as "Mr. World." She gets hold of Mr. World's spear, meant to start the battle that will restore Odin's glory, stands closely in front of him, and plunges the stick into her own body. After

> a moment's resistance—she pushed harder—and the spear pushed into Mr. World. She could feel the warm breath of him on the cool skin of her neck, as he wailed in hurt and surprise, impaled on the spear. (p. 528)

Laura doesn't kill Loki right off, but she weakens him enormously, which buys Shadow enough time to figure out the whole scheme and try to put a stop to it. Once he confronts him, Loki dies too, and waits with Wednesday in the shadows of the netherworld for the battle to resurrect them. Shadow's not going to let this happen, however, so he heads directly to Odin's chosen battle site in hopes of calling the whole thing off.

The End Game

Rock Mountain is located on the Georgia-Tennessee border, somewhere close to Chattanooga. Here, gods of every stripe, similarly duped by Odin, are preparing for battle. In spite of heated passions and fierce rivalries, Shadow manages to talk them down:

> "The battle you came here for isn't something that any of you can win or lose. The winning and the losing are unimportant to him, to them. What matters is that enough of you die. Each of you that falls in battle give him power. Do you understand?" (p. 539)

After some more talking, revealing his now full understanding of the causal events that have led him and them to this place and time, Shadow finally convinces the gods that they, too, have been duped. The gods go home, Odin's plan is thwarted, Laura is laid to rest, and Shadow moves on. Or does he? The novel ends with his visit to Iceland, the original home of the Norse gods, where he encounters the original, Icelandic Odin, who addresses his him in Old Norse on a hillside outside the city. These final moments offer a poignant closure to the narrative, but also leave open the possibility for Shadow's return to the Unites States and the gods he's left behind there, as well as his own status as Balder, "the sweetest-spoken and the most merciful" of the Scandinavian gods.

Whatever the future holds, Shadow's story has tested the limits of determinism in what seems to be a causally dominant world. In this way, his actions express Hume's idea of constant conjunction, which complicates a simple $x \to y$ understanding of derivative causation. Chance, of course, is an important plot device in many literary and cinematic narratives: *The Sting, No Country for Old Men, Rosencrantz and Guildenstern Are Dead*, to name just a few. But *American Gods* is distinct for the way it weaves the con so closely to the truth, and for so long. In its close to six hundred pages, we only find out at the very end that we, like Balder, are victims of a massive scam. And because it expresses the sustained tension that exists between chance and causality, which is frequently dismissed or over-simplified, *American Gods* is on its way—or perhaps even pre-destined—to become a philosophical classic.

2
American Gods Is All Lies!

GREG LITTMANN

American Gods is rightly recognized as a classic of modern fantasy literature, yet fantasy literature itself is often looked down on as an art form. This is strange given that tales of the fantastic, and *especially* fantastic tales of the gods, are by far the *oldest* type of literature. The stories of gods like Enki of the Sumerians, who slew the primordial monster Tiamat, and Horus of the Egyptians, magically conceived by his mother Isis to avenge the murder of his father Osiris, are the earliest stories that we have.

Fantastic tales, and especially tales of the gods, have remained central to human culture ever since. If you wish to have any understanding of the Norse, you must know something of the stories of Odin, how he sacrificed himself to himself on the world tree Yggdrasil to attain knowledge and power. If you wish to have any understanding of modern America, you must know something of the stories of Jesus Christ, how he opened the way to heaven for humanity by sacrificing himself on the cross.

Neil Gaiman Lies about the Gods

Plato hated the fantastic literature of his day, particularly the stories about the gods. ". . . there is an old quarrel between philosophy and poetry" he complained, in his great political tract, the *Republic* (Book X, lines 607b4–5). Philosophy aims to uncover the truth, but the poets are purveyors of falsehoods designed to please their audiences. Plato particularly sets his

sights on Homer, regarded by the ancient Greeks as the greatest poet who had ever lived. Homer's *Iliad* and *Odyssey* are
wild stories of conflicting and conniving gods and goddesses,
astounding monsters, and superhuman heroes who are often,
like Shadow in *American Gods*, themselves part god. As Plato
puts it in his *Ion*,

> Does Homer speak of any subjects that differ from those of *all* the
> other poets? Doesn't he mainly go through tales of war, and of how
> people deal with each other in society. . . . And of the gods, how *they*
> deal with each other and with men? And doesn't he recount what
> happens in heaven and in hell, and tell of the births of gods and
> heroes?" (lines 531c2–d1)

Plato makes the accusation that in composing such fantastic
stories, Homer is commenting on all sorts of subjects on which
he could not possibly be an expert. This is worrying enough
when Homer describes navigational techniques and medical
procedures, but worse yet when he describes such fundamentally important things as the gods and the workings of the
cosmos.

As for *American Gods*, the novel contains nothing *but* falsehoods about the gods. Even if the gods exist, Neil Gaiman, like
Homer before him, is in no position to be an expert about them.
Unless the gods happen to be clueing him in on their conspira-
cies (and if so, I'd like to join), he can't know whether Odin has
a glass eye, or whether Thoth likes coffee cake, or whether the
goddess Bast likes to be scratched behind her ears. Indeed, Neil
Gaiman isn't even *trying* to be truthful—by his own admission,
he just makes all of his fantasy stories up! That Gaiman would
invent stories about the gods for *American Gods* is dreadful
from Plato's point of view, but even more scandalous are the
terrible things that Neil Gaiman's gods *get up to.*

The Gods Shouldn't Be Such Bastards

Plato was particularly horrified by the fact that poets like
Homer so often represented the gods as acting in ways that are
contemptible. To Plato's mind, divine nature must be superior
to human nature, and the acts of the gods must likewise be of
a superior nature. So any tales of the gods in which they act

disgracefully must be lies. Such lies are dangerous since people will see no reason to fear divine judgment for bad behavior if the gods themselves behave badly.

Plato rejects as "the greatest of all lies" the myth related by the poet Hesiod in his _Theogony_ in which the sky god and universal ruler Uranus is castrated and overthrown by his son Cronus, only to be overthrown in turn by his own son, the famous Zeus (_Republic_, Book II, lines 377e5–8). It was unthinkable to Plato that gods would act so unjustly as to overthrow their own fathers and detrimental to public morality for the story to be spread—"Nor should a young person hear it said that in committing the worst crimes he's doing nothing out of the ordinary, or that if he inflicts every kind of punishment on an unjust father, he's only doing the same as the first and greatest of the gods" (lines 378b1–4). Neither should stories be told about "gods warring, fighting, or plotting against one another, for they aren't true" (lines 378b7–c2).

Judged by this standard, _American Gods_ is an appalling piece of literature, about as awful a work of art as Plato could imagine. With a remarkable fidelity to the original mythologies, _American Gods_ is very much a tale of gods behaving badly. Plato criticized Hesiod for writing that the god Cronus overthrew his father, reasoning that no god could do something so unjust. Yet Cronus's crime seems small beer compared to Odin's and Loki's plot to sacrifice the other gods of the United States for their personal benefit. Odin even plans to betray his own son, Shadow, a demi-god who has shown him nothing but loyalty.

The other gods hardly fare any better. The Slavic god Czernobog is a vicious old man whose greatest joy in life is smashing in heads—human heads if possible though animal heads will do in a pinch. The Egyptian god Horus has gone mad, at least partly because he has spent so long living as an animal. Once the ruler of the sky itself, now he is more interested in feasting on road-kill. As for the mysterious "fat kid", representative of the gods of the modern world, he's nothing but a pompous, mentally unbalanced little bully—"Keep your answers short and to the point or I'll fucking kill you. Or maybe I won't kill you. Maybe I'll have the children break every bone in your fucking body. There are two hundred and six of them. So don't fuck with me" (_American Gods_, p. 48).

These deities couldn't be further from Plato's conception of the just and temperate nature of divinity, nor could the story of their actions be further from the sort of god-tales that Plato wanted authors to tell. Perhaps worst of all, the gods are constantly in dispute with one another and, over the course of *American Gods*, even go to war—the old gods against the new. To Plato's mind, the divine influence brings rationality and order and *harmony* to the world. The gods are good, and the good will not conflict with the good. In *American Gods*, on the other hand, the gods are, more often than not, influences that bring madness, chaos and destruction. Indeed, Odin, caring only for war and death, almost leads these foolish deities into annihilating themselves in a final cataclysmic battle.

Gods Shouldn't Eat Road-Kill

Plato also rejects the many stories of divine transformation into animal or other form. He reasons that a god already exists in a superior form and so should be changeless, rather than sometimes choosing to adopt an *inferior* form. It would not be rational to give up a *better* form for a *worse* one. Besides, divine transformation in the stories usually occurs for the sake of deception, and a god would never indulge in anything as base as deception. And so, Plato rejects the tale of Zeus's wife Hera disguising herself as a priestess, so as to trick her husband's lover Semele into making the fatal demand that the god show himself to her in all his divine glory. To Plato's mind, such low trickery is too unworthy of a divine being to be plausible. He states that the gods "are not sorcerers who change themselves, nor do they mislead us by falsehoods in words or deeds" (lines 383a3–4).

Rejecting Plato's advice, the gods in *American Gods* frequently transform into lesser forms. Horus, as just mentioned, has been spending most of his time as a hawk, forsaking his divine body for a lesser, animal body. Meanwhile, his fellow Egyptian Gods Anubis and Bast spend their off-time as a jackal and cat respectively. Media's transformations are weirder still, as she takes on such forms as a black-and-white Lucile Ball and the entire cast of *Cheers*. Indeed, *all* of the gods are pretending to be something that they are not, living secretly among the humans of twenty-first- century America as if they are ordinary humans too.

Plato was upset at Hera being depicted as pretending to be a human priestess, so he would be horrified at *American God's* premise of an underground society comprised of closet deities. Many of these gods can't even be honest with *one another.* Odin and Loki lie to everyone they know almost all of the time, while the other gods are only slightly less deceitful.

Stop Crying, You Sissy God

Furthermore, Plato believed that no sympathetic character should be shown in the grip of extreme emotion, since a soul should be governed by rationality and never overcome by feelings. Even a parent grieving for their child should do their utmost to show no sign of pain. Rather,

> We must accept what has happened as we would the fall of the dice, and then arrange our affairs in whatever way reason determines to be best. We mustn't hug the hurt part and spend our time weeping and wailing like children when they trip. (*Republic*, Book X, lines 604c5–8)

To Plato's mind, characters in fiction should act with restraint and self-discipline, to set us a good example. While Plato's concern was with any extreme display of emotion, he thought it especially bad to convey *gods* and semi-divine heroes succumbing to extreme emotion. This applies even to powerful *positive* emotions such as those involved in having a good laugh—"if someone represents worthwhile people as overcome by laughter, we won't approve, and we'll approve even less if they represent gods that way" (*Republic*, Book III, lines 388e9–389a1).

The gods of *American Gods* do not provide appropriate role-models for us in their mastery of their emotions. They're ruled by their passions at least as much as are we, if not more so. Mad Sweeney is so overcome by despair when he cannot recover the magic gold coin that he gave to Shadow, that he uses the money Shadow gives him for a bus out of town to drink himself into a frozen death. Similarly, Odin's son Thor, Norse god of the storm, "put a gun in his mouth and blew his head off in Philadelphia in 1932" (p. 386) apparently just because he couldn't cope with life anymore.

The old gods as a whole are so easily overcome by battle-lust that they refuse Czernobog's entreaties to consider tactics before assaulting the new gods at Lookout Mountain. "It doesn't matter whether this is a good time or a bad time. This is *the* time" (p.453) announces the Irish war goddess, the Morrigan, and the battle is on. Once again, the gods of the new, and supposedly more rational, age are no better than their ancient counterparts. The "fat kid" is a slave to his own pride, yet collapses into self-destructive hysteria just because he is left alone in a room and doesn't like the solitude—"It sounded like he was throwing something huge against the walls of the room. From the sounds, Shadow guessed that what he was throwing was himself. "It's just me!" he was sobbing" (p. 394).

The gods aren't above having a good laugh, either. Mad Sweeny, Czernobog, Zorya Polunochnaya, Kali, Eostre, Wisekedjak, the all-father Odin, and Anansi are all shown enjoying a laugh. Anansi even tells a funny story about a tiger's balls to a divine crowd at House on the Rock and is well-received—"Mr. Nancy smiled, and bowed his head, and spread his hands, accepting the applause and laughter like a pro, and then he turned and walked back to where Shadow and Czernobog were standing" (p. 122).

Shadow's No Hero

Plato would even condemn Shadow as an inappropriate protagonist. This is so even though Plato would recognize that Shadow has many positive qualities. Shadow is extremely loyal—he may be slow to sign on with Odin, but once his does, he will defend his employer to the death *and even beyond*. Far from being a deceiver by nature, Shadow is so pathologically honest that he is willing to allow Czernobog to crush his head with a massive hammer, rather than to break his promise to the old man. Moreover, Shadow is so restrained in his emotions that he spends almost the entirety of *American Gods* hiding the extreme pain he is in over the infidelity and death of his beloved wife, Laura. As we have seen, Plato recommends that those who have suffered bereavement should conceal their sorrow, keeping a stiff upper lip through self-discipline rather than giving in to their grief. He would surely be impressed, then, by Shadow's stoic endurance in this regard.

However Shadow will sometimes succumb to extreme emotion, including both despair and fear—"He kept climbing, pulling himself up the mountain of skulls, every sharp edge cutting into his skin, feeling revulsion and terror and awe" (p. 268). He's not even above having a *really* good laugh:

> He trapped some water between his bare shoulder and the trunk of the tree, and he twisted his head over and drank the trapped rainwater sucking and slurping at it, and he drank more and he laughed, laughed with joy and delight, not madness, until he could laugh no more, until he hung there too exhausted to move. (p. 412)

Worse yet, Shadow is eventually pushed to the point that, like Cronus and Zeus, he rebels against the rule of his own unjust father. This is *exactly* the sort of thing that Plato didn't think should be depicted and there is no way that Plato could regard Shadow as an appropriately heroic figure.

Given that Shadow is the son of a god, his good behavior would be particularly important to Plato, who has particular concern with the way that the children of deities are shown. Many of the most popular Greek tales were about the half-human sons of gods, and even today we love the adventures of Heracles (aka Hercules), son of Zeus; Theseus, son of Poseidon; and Achilles, son of the nymph Thetis. Plato was critical of many of these tales of demi-gods, insisting that, for the sake of public morals, the relatives of the gods must always be presented as behaving well, as suits their divine heritage. Otherwise, such stories will be

> harmful to people who hear them, for everyone will be ready to excuse himself when he's bad, if he is persuaded that similar things both are being done now and have been done in the past by close descendants of the gods. . . . For that reason, we must put a stop to such stories, lest they produce in the youth a strong inclination to do bad things. (*Republic,* Book III, lines 391e4–392a1)

American Gods Could Corrupt Your Mind

It might be tempting to dismiss the relevance of Plato's criticism of fantastic Greek poetry to modern works like *American Gods*, on the grounds that nobody thinks that *American Gods* represents the world as it really is. That is, it may be objected that people are not going to be misled by a work they understand to be fiction, or corrupted by the example of gods and demi-gods in which they do not believe. However, to Plato's mind, it is a fact of human psychology that art molds us. The mere act of imagining something to be the case as we follow a fictional narrative is enough for the narrative to transform us and we become like the heroes of our narratives. His conception of the effects of art seem akin to that of modern political activists who seek to curb the sexual or violent content in films, for fear that people will embrace the values they see on the screen and replicate the behavior in real life. A modern anti-pornography campaigner will not be mollified by pointing out that a pornographic movie is clearly identified as a work of fiction. The activist believes that such movies put ideas into people's heads, corrupting the morals of viewers and fostering dangerously inaccurate views of women, regardless of whether the movie is formally acknowledged as fiction or not. Similarly, it isn't enough for Plato for stories of gods and heroes acting badly to be acknowledged as fiction. People shouldn't be filling their heads with such nonsense in the first place, for just vividly imagining such things as they listen to the tales will warp their opinions and character. Plato wrote

> And in the case of sex, anger, and all the desires, pleasures, and pains that we say accompany all our actions, poetic imitation . . . nurtures and waters them and establishes them as rulers in us when they out to wither and be ruled. (*Republic*, Book X, lines 606d1–5)

Fantasy Literature Is Garbage and So Is Mythology

American Gods isn't going to rate very highly as art if judged by Plato's standard. The greatest problem with *American Gods* from Plato's point of view is that it is too close to its sources. The gods in *American Gods* just act too much like they did in their original mythologies—more like human beings than the rational and noble deities Plato envisaged.

The Odin of Norse mythology was a lover of battle and slaughter, a bloody god to whom worshippers made human sacrifice. He was a skillful transformer, taking the shape of snake, an eagle, a human being, and presumably any other animal he felt like. He was a liar and deceiver, travelling in disguise and getting his way by guile more often than by force, such as when he stole the magical "mead of inspiration" by tricking the dwarves Fjalar and Galar and seducing the giantess Suttung. This, of course, is just the sort of portrayal of gods in mythology that bothered Plato in the first place—Odin is no better behaved in the North myths than Zeus, Apollo, and Aphrodite are in the Greek myths. To Plato's mind, it's simply no way for a god to behave!

Plato's criticism would extend to fantasy literature in general. Fantasy authors of necessity write about things they know nothing about. Writers like J.R.R. Tolkien and George R.R. Martin describe agricultural communities, though they are not experts on agriculture, and tell of the clashes of great armies armed with swords and spears, though neither writer has ever seen such a battle. Similarly, Gaiman, in writing the television series and novel *Neverwhere*, writes about what it is like to live underground beneath a major city, a subject he can't possibly know a great deal about. Plato would be especially upset to view Gaiman's magnificent episode of *Doctor Who*, "The Doctor's Wife", which, while demonstrating a deep knowledge of the history of the program, fails to demonstrate that the author is any expert on scientific matters.

Particularly problematic, from Plato's point of view, is that fantasy writers write about the *supernatural*, a subject on which they are almost certainly ignorant, yet a subject that Plato thought was extremely important. He believed that the universe was ordered in accordance with rational principles that could be discovered through reasoning about them. When fantasy authors invent the rules by which the universe operates for the purpose of an astounding story, they distract us from the truth about our universe and our place within it. Similarly, the characters in fantasy novels often act in ways of which Plato would disapprove, even if they're divine or divinely inspired.

Tolkien's evil mastermind Sauron was corrupted by the fallen angel Morgoth, which would be an intolerable idea for Plato. A creature of the divine realm must be a pure, rational being, not subject to degenerating into something evil, and the influence of such a creature must improve a human soul, must make it more moral and reasonable. Likewise, the god-like Dream and the other Endless from Neil Gaiman's best-selling

comic book series *Sandman* have no place within Plato's cosmology and would offend him with their self-obsession and
emotional, often irrational, natures, not to mention their love of
transformation and illusion.

Learning to Love Leprechauns

I think you'll agree with me that Plato's missing something
important in his hypothetical review of *American Gods*. Surely
we can devote ourselves to the pursuit of truth, as he recommends, without having to give up *imagining* things being different. I can't accept that we must give up Homer, Hesiod, Neil
Gaiman and all the other poets and writers in history who have
spun fantastic stories about the gods.

One of Plato's students, Aristotle, also wasn't willing to give
up tales of the gods. He didn't believe that they were literally
true any more than Plato did, but could see that they have
value as works of fiction. Aristotle's conception of good fiction
provides a framework for the *appreciation* of *American Gods*.
While we can't be *sure* that Aristotle would have liked the book,
any more than we can be *sure* that Plato would have hated it,
it seems likely that he would at least have recognized its significance as literature.

For a start, Aristotle recognized that there's nothing wrong
with having fun that serves no further purpose. He wrote in his
Politics that it is alright to listen to music just for the sheer
enjoyment of it:

> For the end is not desirable for the sake of any future good, nor do
> the pleasures which we have described exist for the sake of any
> future good but of the past, that is to say, they are the alleviation of
> past toils and pains. And we may infer this to be the reason why men
> seek happiness from these pleasures. (Book VIII, lines 1339b35–40)

As for intellectual pleasures, the sort that stimulate the mind,
he thought that they were essential for a life lived well. He
states: "It is clear . . . that there are branches of learning and
education which we must study merely with a view to leisure
spent in intellectual activity, and these are to be valued for
their own sake" (lines 1338a9–12). *American Gods* is a highly
educated romp through mythology and folklore, a clever game

played by weaving together elements of human culture from across the world and throughout history. By any fair standard, reading such a book must qualify as "leisure spent in intellectual activity", and is thus worthwhile on Aristotle's model.

Moreover, Aristotle appreciated that a story doesn't have to be *true* in order to be worth hearing. In defense of fiction, he wrote in his *Poetics*: "if it be objected that the description is not true to fact, the poet may perhaps reply, 'But the objects are as they ought to be' . . ." or "'This is how men say the thing is'" (line 1460b33–36). He noted that the second reply was particularly appropriate where stories about the gods were involved. Far from rejecting Homer for his wild talks of the gods as Plato did, he wrote that "in the serious style, Homer is pre-eminent among poets" (lines 1448b34–35). Aristotle openly encouraged authors to invent stories and details, calling it "absurd" to "at all costs keep to the received legends" (lines 1451b24–25). The author may instead relate things that *could* happen.

Even the impossible may be included by an author if it makes the story more interesting—"Any impossibilities there are in his descriptions of things are faults. But from another point of view they are justifiable, if they serve the end of poetry—if . . . they make the effect of . . . the work . . . more astounding" (lines 1460b24–26). Aristotle is thus in a position, as Plato was not, to appreciate the need for Mad Sweeney to be able to pull a gold coin from thin air, for a stick to be able to skewer a body as if it were a spear, and for Valaskjalf, hall of the god Odin, to exist in a space accessible only via the carousel at the House on the Rock in Wisconsin. Such things are far beyond possibility, yet these wonders are an essential element of what makes *American Gods* such a striking novel.

Aristotle believed that exposure to fiction can help us learn more about the world than we would if we relied on factual accounts alone. This is because factual accounts, such as are written by historians, can only tell us what *has* happened. Fiction, on the other hand, explores what *could* happen. He wrote: "Hence poetry is something more philosophic and of graver import than history, since its statements are of the nature rather of universals, whereas those of history are singulars" (lines 1451b5–7). In Aristotle's time, most stories were told in verse, so he speaks of 'poetry' when he means any fictional story-telling. Aristotle maintains that if we truly wish to

understand our world and our place within it, it's not enough
to know how things *are*. We also have to understand some of
the alternatives.

Of course, *American Gods* deals with many situations which
are *not* alternatives open to our world—you just *can't* come
back from the dead, no matter how many gold coins you collect,
nor can you ever land a job working for Odin, no matter how
much you might prefer that to whatever you should be doing
now. However, what *American Gods* allows us to do is to consider *characters* in various situations, faced with various
stressful choices, and Aristotle believed that by considering
characters in hypothetical situations, we could learn much
about human nature. We gain insight into ourselves and those
around us by thinking about how a human being is likely to act
in extreme circumstances. Aristotle believed that this is true
even when the story contains divine intervention and other
supernatural elements.

Aristotle was even perfectly happy for characters to exhibit
extremes of emotion. Far from criticizing fictional histrionics,
he thought they served a useful purpose. In his discussion of
tragic theater in the *Poetics*, Aristotle maintained that observing the elaborate lamentations of unfortunate characters in
tragedy purifies our soul of negative emotions. By experiencing
feelings like fear and pity on behalf of the characters on the
stage, we purge ourselves of these very feelings, a process that
Aristotle called "catharsis". Whereas Plato insisted that our
souls would take on the form of the characters presented to us
in art, Aristotle believed that sympathizing with characters in
fiction can vent our emotions, making us *less* like the character, and more like the sort of rational, controlled individuals
that both Plato and Aristotle thought that we should be.

Mad Sweeney cuts a pathetic figure when he confronts
Shadow to beg for the return of the magic gold coin he gave
him. The leprechaun whines and pleads and wallows in hope-
less self-pity—". . . Mad Sweeney just stood there, holding out
his gold-filled cap with both hands like Oliver Twist. And then
tears swelled in his blue eyes and began to spill down his
cheeks" (*American Gods,* p. 218). For Plato, such a display of
weakness, particularly from a divine or semi-divine being,
could only corrupt us. For Aristotle, on the other hand, the pity
we cannot help but feel for Mad Sweeney is good for our souls.

It helps us cope with fear and despair in our own lives when we feel sympathy for this imaginary person.

Fantasy and Rationality in *American Gods*

Fantasy, it is sometimes said, *makes no sense*. The fantasy story, according to this view, defies reason by adopting impossible premises, and so is of no artistic consequence—it can't be *serious* or *important* literature. Aristotle insisted that a good serious story *must* make sense. To be appropriately intellectual entertainment, a story must be rational and events must occur because it is reasonable for them to occur given what has gone before—"the unraveling of the plot, no less than the complication, must arise out of the plot itself" (*Poetics*, lines 1454a38-1454b1). Aristotle likewise held it vital that characterization makes sense:

> The right . . . in the characters just as in the incidents of the play to seek after the necessary or the probable; so that whenever such-and-such a personage says or does such-and-such a thing, it shall be the necessary or probable outcome of his character. (lines 1454a32–36)

However, Aristotle did not believe that the inclusion of fantastic elements within a story interfered with the story making sense in the artistically important way, provided that the implications of the improbable premises unfold in a natural manner. Problems can arise in an unlikely way, provided that they are not resolved in an unlikely way given what has gone before. "There should be nothing improbable among the actual incidents" (line 1454b6). He notes, for instance, that Sophocles's play *Oedipus the King* begins with a divine curse being laid for no obvious reason. That element of the plot is not a rational development of anything that has gone before. However, this is acceptable to Aristotle, because once the improbable premise of *Oedipus the King* has been established, everything else that happens follows in a natural, plausible way. Given the nature of the characters and the situation they find themselves in, they act in accordance with probability.

This, of course, is just the way that *American Gods* is written. The premise—that the ancient gods are real and survive in the modern USA, where they compete with the new gods for human worship—is absurd. Anyone who believed such a thing would be insane. Yet the events of *American Gods* unfold according to an internal logic. Given the characters we're presented with in the situation in which they find themselves, they act as it would be probable for them to act. Shadow remains loyal to Odin because it has always been Shadow's nature to be loyal. Laura sacrifices herself for Shadow because she has always loved Shadow. Conversely, Odin betrays the gods because, in the novel, it has always been Odin's nature to be a selfish grifter.

As Johnny Appleseed advises Shadow, "You don't mind anything your boss says about me. He's an asshole. Always was an asshole. Always goin' to be an asshole. Some people is jes' assholes, and that's an end of it" (p. 200). Even characters who change, like Czernobog, who waits the entire novel to crush Shadow's head with his hammer only to spare his life at the end, change in accordance with their nature. Czernobog's character development seems perfectly natural, given what he and Shadow have been through together.

Other events occur not according the rules of characterization but of mythology. Shadow can gain insight by hanging from a tree for nine days because this is in accordance with the legends of Odin. Mad Sweeney can produce gold from thin air because mysterious access to gold is in accordance with leprechaun folklore. Given the wild premise of *American Gods*, this is exactly the sort of thing that's likely to happen, even though Shadow isn't clued in enough to understand that:

> "These things must be done by the rules," said Czernobog.
> "Yeah," said Shadow. "But nobody tells me what they are. You keep talking about the goddamn rules, I don't even know what game you people are playing." (p. 389)

Even the appearance and actions of new gods like the "fat kid" and Media follow probability, given the sort of creatures that they are. Far from "not making sense", then, *American Gods* makes perfect sense in the way that Aristotle thought was artistically important. Likewise, other works of fantastic fiction may fulfill Aristotle's requirement if they remain true to their premises and if the characters develop in a natural and believable way given the extraordinary circumstances they find themselves in.

We Need Fantastic Stories

The contrast between Plato and Aristotle's views is particularly interesting in that it reflects a division in viewpoints on fantastic literature that persists to this day. Like Plato, many people today look down on fantastic literature on the grounds that it doesn't convey reality. A novel like *American Gods* would be regarded as defective because the things it deals with—gods and magic, for instance—are not *real*. Reading such novels is often condemned with the word "escapism", presumably because the reader is thought to be escaping from the real world.

Plato thought that stories should not convey a false view of the world, and this sentiment seems to be echoed by those who can't regard a work of fantasy as serious or important literature, or even see it as an appropriate use of an adult's time. Plato's view is not entirely divorced from that of those modern Christians who object to fantasy literature on the grounds that it misrepresents the role of God in the universe. Like Plato, such critics are not appeased by the fact that the adventures of Shadow, Gandalf, and all the other characters who don't fit the cosmology are clearly labeled as works of *fiction*. Rather, like Plato, they believe that if people occupy their minds with false ideas regarding religion, they will be corrupted by those ideas.

On the other hand, there are also many people today whose views on fantastic fiction echo those of Aristotle. Like Aristotle, they see nothing wrong with pleasure for pleasure's sake. Reading a novel requires no more justification than that the reader is entertained. Fantastic fiction is thus a worthwhile art form just because people *like it*. Holders of the view may even, like Aristotle, believe that there is particular value in pleasure derived from a clever, intellectual book like *American Gods*. In any case, like Aristotle, those who can see the value of fantasy fiction accept that human beings can maintain a distinction between what they imagine and the way that the world really is. They do not believe that humans will be driven into delusion just by using their imagination to dream of fantastic things. As for fantasy *fans*, they tend to follow Aristotle in desiring their tales of the fantastic to make internal sense. Novels like *American Gods*, in which characters are consistent or develop believably, and in which plot developments follow reasonably from what has gone before, are more highly regarded than novels with clumsy characterization and arbitrary plot development.

I've made no secret of where I stand on all of this. People who condemn fantastic literature like *American Gods* for being set so far from reality are failing to understand some significant facts about the nature of *art*. As Aristotle appreciated, if you're enjoying a work of art while doing no harm, then you are using art correctly—to be enjoyed is a legitimate function of art. Moreover, as Aristotle understood, if art is stimulating your intellect, then you're using art correctly—the pure exercise of thinking and imagining is good for you.

Finally, as we are in a much better position to see than Aristotle was, fantastic tales are a central and ineliminable element of human culture. Fantastic stories are found in every culture and the adventures of the gods almost always play a central role.

Before Odin was conning the other gods into a grand sacrifice at Lookout Mountain, he was killing the giant Ymir to make the world, and presiding over the souls of dead warriors in his hall Valhalla. Before Kali was bickering with Odin in the House on the Rock, she was slaying the demon Raktabija by sucking out his blood, and dancing so energetically that she was in danger of destroying the world. Before Anansi was breaking Shadow out of prison in Lakeside while disguised as a police deputy, he was creating the sun and moon, and teaching the art of agriculture to humanity.

American Gods stands as part of an ancient and universal literary tradition. To reject the need for such stories is to fail to appreciate something fundamental about humans and human culture.

3
To Survive, You Must Believe

RAY BOSSERT

In *American Gods*, Gaiman creates a series of supernatural characters who embody the essence of particular aspects of American culture. He imagines a god of American media, a god of American electronic communications, even a goddess of American liberty. So, which of Gaiman's characters is the god of American Philosophy?

There isn't one.

At least, there doesn't seem to be a particular god you can point to and say: "Ah, he represents how they do philosophy in the United States." The conspicuous absence of such a god could just be the best representation of American Philosophy, a field whose practitioners sometimes describe themselves as feeling lost in the shuffle of American life. Compare the storyline of *American Gods* with the following quote about the state of philosophy:

> Some think that we are floundering, not knowing what to do next. Some think that what we are doing is waiting for another generation of major figures (new Quines, Rawlses, &c.), rather like Heidegger's telling us *that we need a god*. And there are a few, very few, I guess, like me, who think that this isn't such a bad thing, because we think that at least one kind of real philosophy requires always starting over, never taking anything for granted or as given. (italics added)

The reviewer, Ted Cohen of the University of Chicago, inadvertently summarizes the entire story arc of Gaiman's novel in these three sentences. Shadow begins his quest with his world in utter upheaval—he has discovered his wife is dead on the day he is released from prison and the job he thought was waiting for him is gone. Shadow, quite literally, doesn't have a clue what to do next.

Direction, however, is offered in the form of Wednesday, a seemingly wandering grifter who turns out to be a manifestation of the Norse god Odin. But by the end Shadow discovers that the supernatural journey he had embarked upon was in fact a ruse—he finds himself having to question everything he thought he had learned and start all over again. He didn't believe in gods when the novel started. "Shadow was not superstitious" (p. 6), and he was skeptical of the gods even when he met them. (Professor Cohen, coincidentally, describes a "healthy skepticism" as a hallmark of American thinking.) That skepticism turns out to be fairly useful when the gods turn out not to be what people think they should be.

Intellectualism Is Not American

France. November 10th, 1793. The French Convention, having rebelled against the monarchy and drastically reduced the height of numerous *Monsieurs* and *Madames*, declared a new state religion under the Goddess of Reason, that is Sophia. Evidently, French Philo-sophia (the love of wisdom) is ardent enough to become a national idolatry. Had Neil Gaiman written *French Gods*, he would have had a ready-made, native French Goddess of Philosophy at his disposal.

While the French have offered fewer decapitated heads to their rational Goddess in recent years, their pride and interest in their philosophy seems no less passionate. On the death of Jean-Paul Sartre, thousands—some reports go as high as fifty thousand—paid their respects at his memorial in 1980. This means he might have garnered almost as many mourners at his funeral as Elvis Presley in Memphis three years earlier (about eighty thousand people came out for The King). The French love their philosophers about as much as Americans love their rock stars.

It's not just a French thing either. American philosophical circles widely and enviously disseminate a belief that philosophy is a fairly mainstream topic of conversation throughout most of Europe. Consider this depressing depiction of America from the *Internet Encyclopedia of Philosophy* (a self-proclaimed peer-reviewed source, so you can cite it in undergraduate papers):

> Unlike European cultures, there has tended to be less of an academic class in America, hence less of a sense of professional philosophy, until, that is, the twentieth century. Even then, much of what has been taken as philosophy by most Americans has been distant from what most professional philosophers have taken as philosophy. The kind of public awareness in France and indeed Europe as a whole of, say, the death of Jean-Paul Sartre, was nowhere near matched in America by the death of Quine, though for professional philosophers the latter was at least of equal stature. Few American philosophers have had the social impact outside of academia as John Dewey.

You get the impression that Europeans engage in philosophy like another form of mass-media entertainment, like movies, books, or soccer . . . er . . . football.

In the United States of America, not so much.

So you could read *American Gods* as a sort of allegory for the state of American Philosophy. I'm not suggesting that Gaiman intends us to read his story this way, merely that there are some uncanny parallels between the way Gaiman depicts the gods and the way philosophy functions in American life. The American gods are like American philosophers in that both groups operate in the background of society and behind the scenes. American philosophy is often accused of not exerting enough pressure in the public realm, for instance, by explicitly making political or social statements.

This isn't to say that individual philosophers don't make their political opinions known, and I'm certainly not saying that American philosophy doesn't influence American politics, but most Americans would be hard-pressed to identify such influences by name. In this regard, American philosophers are quite like Gaiman's American gods whose existence lies largely hidden from society: they veil their influence from public sight. An individual has to possess specialized knowledge, he or she has to be "in the know" in order to recognize the influence of a god or a philosopher.

Any number of accounts of American philosophy describe it as being almost exclusively an academic affair, written for an audience of tenured colleagues and (with the exception of the volume now in your hands) hardly ever taking time to play outside with other kids. The philosopher credited for being the most socially-well-adjusted is John Dewey who (despite being popularly mistaken for the inventor of the Dewey Decimal system) took pains to address his brand of philosophy to the workaday American and to apply his philosophy in ways that could directly affect public opinion and public policy.

Keeping It Real

The lack of interest in philosophy often leads to assumptions that Americans are "anti-intellectual." And this may in fact be the case, as seems evident in Shadow's prison life. At one point, Loki, going by the anglicized name Lyesmith, tries to convince Shadow to read the classical Greek historian Herodotus:

> Lyesmith had loaned Shadow a battered paperback copy of Herodotus's *Histories* several months earlier. "It's not boring. It's cool," he said, when Shadow protested that he didn't read books. (p. 6)

Shadow doesn't read, and Loki's approach to convincing Shadow to read has all of the desperation of a high school teacher trying to seem relevant to today's youth: "It's cool." The Loki doth protest too much. Not only does Loki have to sell Shadow on Herodotus, Gaiman finds it necessary to explain Herodotus to *us*, the readers of the American book market.

In another scene from prison that juxtaposes the intellectual with the anti-intellectual, Shadow reminisces about Johnnie Larch, a prisoner who had served his time but found himself unable to manage life outside of prison. After gaining his liberty, Johnnie promptly finds himself re-incarcerated. This is the wisdom Johnnie has gained from his brief adventure outside of prison:

> And the moral of this story, according to Johnnie Larch, was this: don't piss off people who work in airports.
>
> "Are you sure it's not something like 'The kind of behavior that works in a specialized environment, such as prison, can fail to work and in fact become harmful when used outside such an environment'?" said Shadow, when Johnnie Larch told him the story.

"No, listen to me, I'm *telling* you, man," said Johnnie Larch, "don't piss off those bitches in airports." (pp. 15–16)

In this exchange, Shadow sounds like an eggheaded academic philosopher, using academic jargon like "specialized environment." Shadow attempts to construct a broader, philosophical interpretation of Johnnie's experience, but Johnnie's version is more practical, one might even say pragmatic. In this sense, Johnnie embodies American pragmatism—a philosophy that is less concerned with unveiling what is "Truth" than it is with understanding what is useful. Determining whether complex dynamics of social behaviors depend on environmental context, and then trying to unfold the implications of such an interrelation in a given situation is not as useful to a recently released prisoner as straight-talking advice not to annoy service workers.

This kind of pragmatism is voiced again later in the novel, when Shadow picks up a temporary sidekick in the wandering young woman, Sam. Sam suspects that Shadow might have killed some special agents (who were actually victims of his zombified wife). Concerned about her safety, she confronts Shadow and demands:

"Just tell me you're one of the good guys."

"I can't," said Shadow. "I wish I could. But I'm doing my best."

She looked up at him, and bit her lower lip. Then she nodded. "Good enough," she said. "I won't turn you in. You can buy me a beer." (p. 396)

Sam wants to see the world with a simple good-guy–bad-guy pragmatism. When Shadow complicates this worldview, she settles for the most simple truth she can get. The phrase "good enough" takes on particular significance for the cognitive theorist Ellen Spolsky. Applying Darwin's theory of natural selection to the systems of human thought, Spolsky writes:

The only 'goal' we can speak of with reference to adaptation is species survival. . . . This does not mean that everyone has to understand everything or that understanding is a logically water-tight, foolproof system. All it has to be is *good enough*. (p. 301, Spolsky's italics)

It isn't just humans that rely on questionable but "good enough" logic. At one point, Shadow reflects when talking to the new gods: "Still, these people seemed to like clichés" (p. 437). The new gods reflect modern American preferences for distilling reality into quick, easy-to-remember soundbites that are not necessarily perfect reflections of reality. Shadow seems to acknowledge this with an elitist snobbery. Clichés seem cheap, vulgar, oversimplified. But they also get the job done. They might not always be true, but they are often *true enough*.

Survival of the Fittest Philosophy

When philosophers think about how useful a way of looking at the world is, they start thinking about worldviews as tools, leading to the philosophical concept known as "instrumentalism." Some philosophers claim that instrumentalism is distinctly American, at that. In an essay "Why American Philosophy? Why Now?" Larry A. Hickman writes:

> The American philosophy that I know is deeply rooted in the history of its native country. That is not to say that it somehow began from scratch, that nothing has been imported from abroad. When the Puritans came to New England in the seventeenth century, for example, they brought with them ideas and practices that had been influenced by their time in England and the Netherlands. But they were very soon faced with new conditions which demanded that old tools, the conceptual ones as well as the tangible ones that fit their hands, be modified for the new environment and the new tasks they faced.

Hickman thinks about the origins of American philosophy as being rooted in its European ancestry. Gaiman reminds us of this when Wednesday says "Nobody's American. . . . Not originally. That's my point" (p. 105). In this way, American philosophy is quite like Gaiman's American gods—the oldest forms are imports. However, the old systems give way to the new—and the new, as Hickman points out, is based on usefulness and survival.

Themes of survival run throughout the novel. During one of Shadow's early dreams, the buffalo man offers Shadow the following advice:

"Believe," said the rumbling voice. "If you are to survive, you must believe."

"Believe what?" asked Shadow. "What should I believe?" . . .

"*Everything*," roared the buffalo man. (p. 18)

The buffalo man doesn't offer this advice to stimulate Shadow's curiosity. The buffalo man doesn't exhort belief as a means of achieving some kind of higher spiritual plane, or expand one's intellectual capacity. The buffalo man tells Shadow to believe because his *survival* depends upon it.

At the other end of the novel, Shadow finds himself part of an ancient ritualistic sacrifice to Odin: Shadow hangs to death from a tree. Again in a quasi-dream state, Shadow receives advice from supernatural sources: "The hardest part is simply surviving" (p. 435); and "*It's easy*, said someone in the back of his head. *There's a trick to it. You do it or you die*" (p. 458). Again, Shadow's participation in the ritual is not about Enlightenment or transcending the mortal world; it's about survival—both Wednesday's and his own. His suffering serves as part of Wednesday's resurrection. Rituals, in this scene, are tools of survival. However, the ritual itself is not the only tool at work. Those who participate in the ritual are also objectified:

"Who am I?" asked Shadow.

"You?" said the man. "You were an opportunity. You were part of a grand tradition. Although both of us are committed enough to the affair to die for it. Eh?" (p. 435)

The answer Shadow receives does not answer "who" he is as a person, but "what" he is as a thing. According to Hickman, instrumentalism looks at everything in terms of tools for survival and looks at how new tools can be crafted to survive in a changing world. These tools might be literal, in terms of looking at a clump of iron ore and seeing the raw ingredients of a hammer (and think how often old gods like Czernobog are associated with hammers), or, more significantly, they might be philosophical: such as seeing how systems of thinking like religion or laws might help us survive. Gaiman's American gods exhibit exactly this instrumentalist philosophy because their primary dramatic conflict in the novel is precisely one of survival. Their pragmatic quest to be believed "just enough" leads them towards an instrumentalist view of their world.

We discover Wednesday is Shadow's father, but Wednesday does not perceive Shadow so much as a son as a tool, an instrument by which he can forge his own means of survival.

> "You needed a son," said Shadow.
>
> Wednesday's ghost-voice echoed. "I need *you*, my boy. Yes. My own boy. I knew that you had been conceived, but your mother left the country. It took us so long to find you. And when we did find you, you were in prison. We needed to find out what made you tick. What buttons we could press to make you move. Who you were." (pp. 533-34)

Ultimately, Wednesday and Loki perceive the other gods the same way. But this, of course, is also how humans more or less view the gods. According to the narrative, gods manifest out of human needs. Gods are like any other survival tool. We craft them like axes, arrows, and fire. As society marches through time, however, some tools are more useful than others. In the twenty-first century the average human has little use for the tools that were once necessary. Czernobog's hammer gives way to Media's television set. Now, an individual's survival in a first-world economy depends far more on one's ability to communicate electronically than it does on the ability to produce and manipulate fire or kill food.

Gods, Gaiman would suggest, served a need, if only as a tool for maintaining social order. Gods represented relationships between human beings as well as between human beings and their environment. Those relationships, in the fiction, became literally "real" entities. As those relationships evolved, so too do the entities that embody them. But not all relationships evolve—some go extinct.

Goodbye Jupiter; hello Google.

In a dramatic speech that he hopes will persuade the gods to abandon their cataclysmic war, Shadow says:

> This is a bad land for gods. . . . You've probably all learned that, in your own way. Old gods are ignored. The new gods are as quickly taken up as they are abandoned, cast aside for the next big thing. Either you've been forgotten, or you're scared you're going to be rendered obsolete,

or maybe you're just getting tired of existing on the whim of people. (p. 538)

Shadow describes the gods' collective fear of becoming "obsolete," a word that people usually apply to tools and instruments like computers, or cell phones, or operating systems like last year's version of Microsoft Windows. Religion is an operating system for dealing with the world, and, like other operating systems, religions need updates to stay compatible with new software and hardware.

Liberty, Independence, and Lonely Professors

When Shadow delivers his concluding remarks to the gods on the cusp of their war, he expresses a desire for independence: "I think I would rather be a man than a god. We don't need anyone to believe in us. We just keep going anyhow. It's what we do" (p. 539). Shadow wants to be beholden to no one, neither human nor god. He wants to exist as an individual entity. He desires a private life. The gods, too, reflect this sentiment. One reason why the American gods seem invisible to the world is because they often work in isolation. They focus on their own sphere of influence, privately.

Late in the novel, the Egyptian deity Mr. Ibis talks about the precision with which gods have their roles defined:

> We all have so many functions, so many ways of existing. In my own vision of myself, I am a scholar who lives quietly, and pens his little tales, and dreams about a past that may or may not ever have existed. And that is true, as far as it goes. But I am also, in one of my capacities, like so many of the people you have chosen to associate with, a psychopomp. I escort the living to the world of the dead. (pp. 479–480)

Mr. Ibis depicts himself as an academic, a "scholar" thinking in isolation about the way things are or might have been. But even in his other role as "psychopomp," he sounds like an academic—for what else does a teacher do than escort living pupils to the realm of thinkers long gone?

Ibis is not just a scholar of anything, though. The gods have specialized functions. In the *City of God*, St. Augustine once noted that the Romans believed that a single god existed for almost everything the human mind could imagine. The same is a commonplace complaint among critics of the American academy. Looking at the philosophy department of an American university or college, you'll find philosophers specializing in aesthetics, politics, cognitive theory, ethics (normative and practical), epistemology, mathematical logic, analytic philosophy, philosophy of particular historical periods, philosophy of specific geographic or ethnic origins, philosophy of (the mind, history, language, science, insert favorite topic here in the Mad Libs approach to academic research) . . . the list goes on. One can even become a philosopher specializing in the philosophy of other philosophers.

While classical, ancient pantheons certainly shared this type of specialization, their gods were typically more social. In Gaiman's novel, most gods are loners. They might live in small communities, like the nuclear families in the cases of the Eastern European or Egyptian gods, but they are not a vast community like the Olympians. They don't share condo units in a high-rise named Valhalla. Gaiman's American gods typically pursue happiness as individuals, working together collectively only when necessary. Even in the quote above, Mr. Ibis expresses a freedom to imagine himself in a way distinct from his official capacity. To a certain extent, Mr. Ibis resists having his role completely defined for him.

Their specializations also reflect the American ideal of the right "to pursue happiness." In the American Declaration of Independence, "happiness" is classically defined on a philosophical premise. It's more than just epicurean delight or pleasure. It's a fulfillment of one's self-perceived purpose. The American gods are far more free than their predecessors to revel in their own spheres, so long as their spheres have minimal detriment to the humans with which they coexist. Once again we see the parallel with contemporary American philosophy. Philosophers are not exactly in high demand in popular culture (present company excluded). Yet, every year, I teach students who major in philosophy and who talk to me about applying to graduate programs in philosophy. The right "to pursue happiness" inspires and enables students to follow intellectual pursuits for their own sake. There are limits to this freedom, such as economic barriers, but my point is that a proportion of American youth opt to live in an obscure, shadow world of mental constructs. They can only do this because they are at liberty to make this choice for themselves.

American Gods does not always present such liberty as a good thing, though:

> "Lady Liberty," said Wednesday. "Like so many of the gods that Americans hold dear, a foreigner. In this case a Frenchwoman, although in deference to American sensibilities, the French covered up her magnificent bosom on the statue they presented to New York. Liberty," he continued, wrinkling his nose at the used condom that lay on the bottom flight of steps, toeing it to the side of the stairs with distaste—"Someone could slip on that. Break his neck" he muttered, interrupting himself. "Like a banana peel, only with bad taste and irony thrown in." He pushed open the door, and the sunlight hit them. "Liberty . . . is a bitch who must be bedded on a mattress of corpses . . . a bitch who liked to be fucked on the refuse from the tumbril. Hold your torch as high as you want to, m'dear, there's still rats in your dress and cold jism dripping down your leg." (pp. 104–05)

This American struggle between liberty and its limits is at the heart of Gaiman's novel. Gaiman plays a joke on liberty in the middle part of Wednesday's speech. The used condom in this passage reflects both the value and the cost of liberty; it disrupts Wednesday's speech, but also becomes a feature of it. If delivered in film, we would hear the actor say "Liberty—someone could slip on that. Break his neck." Liberty is double-edged; the freedom to succeed is also the freedom to fail.

Still, Wednesday's pessimistic depiction of liberty might stem from his god-function. He is the ultimate patriarch, the All-Father, the Scandinavian Chieftain-Lord who commands. Liberty among subordinates is not something that an ancient ruler typically values. The sexual liberty implied by the used condom conveys how quickly liberty can devolve into a chaotic libertine lifestyle, and chaos is the very thing that a Norse god attempts to hold off as long as possible. Although Wednesday himself is hardly chaste, Wednesday's view of sexuality as a manifestation of the All-Father cannot merely be the hedonism of the libertine. For Wednesday, sexual activity serves a purpose, a function to perpetuate life (Gaiman depicts Wednesday's sexuality as being vampiric) or in the sense of reproduction. A used condom represents a sexual freedom at the cost of biological function; contraception prevents fatherhood—which thus threatens Wednesday as a manifestation of idealized fatherhood.

Shadow, in any event, seems unpersuaded by Wednesday, proclaiming of Liberty, "I think she's beautiful" (p. 105). Shadow's love of Liberty is perhaps the biggest obstacle to Wednesday's schemes. When Wednesday first offers Shadow a job, Shadow refuses: "I'm going home. I've got a job waiting for me there. I don't want any other job" (p. 22). Shadow has his own plans, and he won't be told to follow another's. Later, after Shadow dies on the tree, he faces a trial before the American-Egyptian pantheon. Classically, depictions of the Egyptian death trial show a feather, representing one's deeds, placed on a scale. According to Gaiman's fictionalized cosmology: "If the feather balances . . . you get to choose your own destination" (p. 483). Shadow, though no saint, proves good enough to squeak by the test.

> Shadow said, "So now I get to choose where I go next?"
> "Choose," said Thoth. "Or we can choose for you."
> "No," said Shadow. "It's okay. It's my choice." (p. 483)

Apparently, the Egyptian gods offer Shadow the opportunity to construct his own afterlife, and the afterlife Shadow chooses for himself is nothingness. Suffice to say, Gaiman has taken some liberties with ancient Egyptian theology in which the good soul continued to exist in the actual world but was granted access to some previously exclusive god-clubs. In Gaiman's novel, however, the reward for a good life is not VIP access to the universe but ultimate liberty—the liberty to define your reality completely and independently. The gods have been Americanized: freedom and independence are their greatest gift to humanity.

4
American Monads

RICHARD ROSENBAUM

In Neil Gaiman's novel, *American Gods*, all the figures of ancient myth are real and still hanging around in modern society; plus, a crop of *new* gods have appeared, gods of Television and the Internet and so on.

As Mr. Wednesday, an incarnation of the Norse god Odin, likes to say, a storm is coming: war is brewing between the old gods and the new over which worldview, and therefore which pantheon, will gain supremacy in the American psyche leaving the other to be forgotten and fade away.

Also some guy gets eaten by a lady's vagina. Anyway, as it turns out, *gods need prayer badly*. A god is created as the representation of a concept when a large enough group of humans believe in what it represents, and it continues to exist only through the persistence of those beliefs. Without believers, living gods will disappear from reality, making the quest for worshippers in a world of declining belief a matter of life and death for Mr. Wednesday and his team.

As the plot of an urban fantasy, especially in the hands of a writer as talented as Gaiman, it's a tremendous premise. But beyond that, it also takes concepts from philosophy—amalgamating ancient and modern ideas—and uses them to create the rules of the novel's world that are not just logical and consistent but in a strange way *believable*, telling us, in the process, a lot about how our real world works.

Plato's Fun Factory

At a time when belief in the mythological gods was still in full swing and totally mainstream, the philosopher Plato promoted the idea of *Forms*. Platonic Forms are the universal concepts underlying every specific physical instance of a thing. A good example is a circle: you can draw a circle and recognize that it's a circle, even though it's impossible to draw something that's *perfectly* circular. In fact, no one has ever *seen* a Perfect Circle (unless you're talking about the rock band by that name, which you should really check out if they're coming to your town, because they're awesome). Any physical representation of a circle is bound to be at least slightly imperfect because imperfection is the nature of the physical world. Nevertheless, the *concept* of a circle is one that everyone inherently recognizes—everyone knows what a circle is, despite having never seen an ideal one.

Plato explains that Forms exist outside of space and time, beyond the physical world that we inhabit. The Form of a circle is its eternal essence, in a sense its soul. The gods of American Gods are similar to Plato's Forms. Each god represents a specific aspect of existence—to the Norse, Odin represented battle, wisdom, and victory, among other things. With the new gods of Gaiman's novel, Media, for instance, represents—uh, like, *media*.

Forms are concepts that exist beyond the scope of any individual person, and of which you can point to examples but never to the actual thing itself. Ancient mythology did this kind of thing a lot—making a character out of an abstract concept and using it as a narrative device to play around with in stories.

We could look at *American Gods* that way, as pure allegory the way that many myths function, and it does work on that level. But it's also more complex than that. Plato emphasizes that Forms aren't something you can find anywhere in the physical world; they're purely abstract objects. And yet in *American Gods*, you have Odin and Media and Anansi (African spider-god and trickster) walking around the United States like they own the place, side-by-side with actual human beings who are simply people and don't represent anything except themselves.

Not only that, but the plot of the novel hinges on the fact that it's the beliefs of humans that keep the gods alive, and if their believers disappear, so do the gods; surely Plato would say that the Forms exist independently of anyone's awareness of them or belief in them. The Circle doesn't disappear from the World of Ideas even if there aren't any people around to draw circles or whatever. Something else is obviously going on here.

Three Worlds, Three Mysteries

The concept of Platonic Forms has been adopted and modified by many different thinkers throughout the centuries.

Psychologist Carl Jung wrote about the very similar idea of *archetypes*—symbols that are common across all human minds and cultures, and tend to be anthropomorphized through storytelling—which is maybe a more precise way to talk about the gods and other figures of mythology.

Roger Penrose (physicist and author of, among others, the fascinating and baffling thousand-page tome *The Road to Reality*, modestly subtitled *A Complete Guide to the Physical Universe*) considers himself a follower of Plato too; much like the Pythagoreans (a sort of math cult existing during Plato's time), Penrose considers numbers to be real things, in the sense that they exist independently from anything they might happen to enumerate. Yet Penrose also sees a connection between the world of Platonic Forms and the world of Physical Objects—and also the world of human Minds, which is where we can see the *American Gods* connection most strongly.

Penrose gives us this picture of the three worlds and the relationship between them:

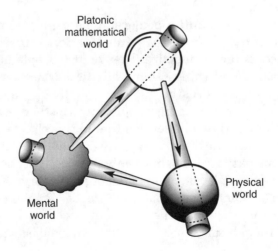

We see here the interconnectedness (and perhaps the interdependence) of the three spheres of existence that Penrose calls the Physical World, the Mental World, and the Platonic Mathematical World (although he admits that the Platonic Forms could very well apply to non-mathematical objects as well, such as aesthetics and morality, or, presumably, television and lightning and Egyptians with carnivorous genitalia). These three worlds are equally real, though each in its own different way.

The Physical World is the one in which we live—or at least in which our bodies live—but, curiously, it is a world that scrupulously obeys rules that are objective and not themselves really physical at all, but purely mathematical.

The Mental World, Penrose says, is a state that comes about in association with certain physical structures. Consciousness (the mind) is somehow produced by the operations of the brain, even though the brain is physical and consciousness is not physical. And the mind is capable of apprehending directly the ideal objects of the Platonic World, so that you can draw a circle and everyone will recognize it as an imitation of the Circle as it exists as a perfect Form.

This sort of mutual confluence between the three worlds gives us a bit of insight into how Odin and that lot can inhabit the physical realm in *American Gods*, and also what human belief might have to do with it. The mind has a certain kind of access to the World of Forms and a certain degree of efficacy when it comes to translating those Forms into physical impressions.

The gods—the anthropomorphic personifications—that we encounter in *American Gods* aren't perfect representations of the concepts they symbolize. They're also people made of flesh and blood, doing things that Platonic Forms obviously don't do—they eat and breathe and occasionally die, and sometimes they devour unsuspecting supplicants via their womanly bits (that's the last time I'll mention that in this chapter, I promise). So they're not the Forms themselves, but still just imperfect reflections of those concepts—only physically embodied.

We can think of Plato's famous Allegory of the Cave, wherein a number of people live inside a cave, permanently chained there so that they can only ever see a single wall. Behind them burns a perpetual fire; when objects pass in front of the fire, the only part of the objects that the people can observe, and which they therefore end up believing is the actual nature of the objects (because they have no idea that anything beyond the cave even exists), are the objects' *shadows* cast on the cave wall. Thought of in this sense, we can better understand how the gods of *American Gods* can be concepts but still have the appearance of physical beings—and it also gives a whole new dimension to the symbolism of the protagonist, who acts as a sort of go-between for the world of the gods and the world of humans and whose name is, of course, Shadow.

Simply Delicious

But the gods of the novel aren't mathematical concepts or drawings of circles. Is there a philosophical theory that could suggest a mechanism for how the theology of *American Gods* works, how Forms can become people through the power of human belief? You can tell the answer is yes, because this chapter goes on for a few more pages.

The philosopher and mathematician Gottfried Leibnitz (not to be confused with Gilbert Gottfried . . . although, what the hell, go ahead and confuse them if you want) formulated a metaphysical theory in a short but dense work called *Monadology*, which may be able to bridge the gap between Platonic forms and physical incarnation that *American Gods* presents. Notably, Leibniz and his contemporary Sir Isaac Newton both developed the mathematical system of calculus simultaneously and completely independently of one another, and their rivalry continues to this very day via the brands of cookies named in their honor: Fig Newtons, and Choco Leibniz. Seriously, that is a real thing.

Leibniz described monads as the ultimate components of reality. Simple, unique and indivisible, monads are the most fundamental building blocks of the universe. They are not themselves physical but they can combine into "compounds" to form physical objects (a little like Voltron), so that everything that exists is, at its core, made up of monads. "Everything that exists" would include, of course, not just the physical world, but also the mental world and the world of Platonic Forms—and Leibniz's monadology has often been described as a modernized version of Plato's theory of Forms.

So every Form, just like every body, could also be thought of as a monad or a bunch of monads. In the parlance of our times, you could say that quarks are on some deep level made out of monads, but so are ideas. Therefore minds and bodies and Forms are not fundamentally different in terms of substance but only in structure, which would make the transformation from one into the other a much simpler matter than if they were all composed of utterly distinct elements.

The idea that everything is made from a single type of substance has been dubbed *monism*. Its direct opposite would be *dualism*, which was the prevailing philosophical position in Leibniz's time, and most famously promoted by René Descartes, which held that the mind and body are composed of two completely different substances and interact in some mysterious way that nobody could really figure out.

Monism gets around that mind-body interaction problem by eliminating dualism altogether, making interaction a non-issue. What's probably the most popular framework among philosophers today is another form of monism called *materialism* or *physicalism*, which is pretty much exactly what it says on the tin: that everything that exists can be reduced to purely physical components, also getting rid of the need for the interaction between two inherently incompatible substances. Leibniz's monism would be called *idealism* since it posits that mental properties—or at least non-physical properties—are fundamental.

Beyond their simplicity and indivisibility, Leibniz's monads have another interesting element, which is that they're *alive*. Sort of. Monads have inherent mental properties, which Leibniz calls *perception* and *appetition*. Perceptions are internal, subjective impressions of some kind of sensory information—thoughts, emotions, sensations, and so on.

Appetitions are the links that chain perceptions together, the causal forces that act to move from one state of perception to the next one. Monads aren't necessarily conscious, but contain stuff that can agglomerate into consciousness. A bare monad has perceptions but won't know that it does, because it's not conscious. At the next level up, a monad gains a capacity to recollect its perceptions, at which point it has consciousness and becomes a *soul*. And at the highest level it gains *apperception*—perception of perception, or a sort of metaperception or self-awareness—and then it becomes, in Leibniz's framework, a *spirit*.

A person's central monad, the sort of centre of gravity of his or her identity, is such a spirit. Surrounded by countless other monads at lower levels all clustered together into the physical particles that make up the body, transmitting perceptions up and down to the central monad, which transmits appetitions that control their behavior.

It sort of goes against our natural assumptions to consider things having mental states but not consciousness, but that's what Leibniz tells us the world is like. It's an idea you can get used to if you spend enough time thinking about it. And it goes a long way to explaining how something could be a person and also lightning at the same time, like in *American Gods*, in that lightning could have some sort of mind or mind-like capacity, and it also explains how mental events can affect physical ones—they're all just monads, connected by appetitions.

You can see how the appearance in a human mind of a belief—which is a thought, which is a monad—that adheres to other similar belief-monads from the minds of other people, could in this way "level up" and develop its own soul, its own spirit. Its own consciousness.

That's what Jung would call an archetype existing in the *Collective Unconscious* of humanity, the storehouse of images and ideas common across all minds, that Plato and Penrose would place in the World of Forms.

How does that translate, though, from a completely non-physical Form into a Mr. Wednesday who can chat with Shadow and hire him as a bodyguard? One more step can get us there.

Godmodding

The Australian philosopher David J. "Superintendent" Chalmers gives us a very similar idea to Leibniz's when he talks about the "hard problem of consciousness" in his book *The Conscious Mind*. The hard problem is basically just the seemingly intractable question of how the subjective character of consciousness can possibly be reduced to purely physical phenomena, or, in simpler terms, "What the hell, consciousness?"

Chalmers concludes that consciousness *can't* be reduced, and suggests that we might just have to take mental properties as fundamental (much as we take physical properties like mass or concepts like causality as fundamental) and start looking into what the rules for the interaction of mind and matter are instead. In taking mental properties as basic, Chalmers admits that this might mean that everything has some sort of mind to it, or at least something mind-like. Just the way that Leibniz suggests. Chalmers calls this *panprotopsychism*; the idea that everything is *potentially conscious* if assembled in just the right way.

At the same time, Chalmers appeals to Information Theory, which suggests that the most basic component of the universe, out of which everything else is built, is *information*. Which is kind of a self-serving theory—it might be more interesting if Information Theory said that everything was made out of *not* information, but, like, some kind of orangey foam But there you go.

Anyway, it seems as if there's no real reason why Leibniz would object to his monads being described as informational in nature. Information, therefore, would have to have inherent mental properties. Which is interesting in itself, but what's more interesting is that according to Chalmers, information has two aspects—physical and phenomenal (or mental) and they're interdependent.

Whenever there's information that's realized phenomenally it's also going to be realized physically. So that if, let's say, a shared belief across millions of human minds—which is certainly information, and according to this reading, a monad—if it's something that exists as an independent entity like a soul or spirit rather than a bunch of isolated perceptions inside individuals' brains—it's going to *become physical*. It *has to*. That's just the nature of the thing, it's one of those psychophysical laws that Chalmers urges thinkers to start looking for.

Neil Gaiman found it. In the storyworld of *American Gods*, the universe is *made* from thoughts, information, monads, and as the human mind absorbs experience and manufactures understanding, it gives birth to gods. There's no choice in the matter, that's simply how the universe in which Shadow finds himself functions.

How different from that universe is the one that we actually live in? Who knows? That's just what philosophers from Chalmers through Leibniz, all the way back to Plato have been

trying to discover. Neil Gaiman, of course, is in the same busi-
ness of interrogating the world and its stories to see how it
works, through narrative rather than pure reason—although
Plato would have hated *American Gods*. It wasn't anything
personal, but in his book *The Republic* he expressed his convic-
tion that since the only *real* world was the World of Forms, with
the Physical World being just its pale shadow, then art, as nothing more than a flawed copy of the flawed copy, is inherently
two degrees removed from Ultimate Reality and therefore
worse than useless for anyone attempting to understand the
truth about the universe.

So look, nobody's perfect.

What You See

5
Living in the Dreamworld

T. Bradley Richards

You are awakened after a long period in cryogenic stasis and are told that, in the super-technological future world you have now arrived in, people regularly enjoy traveling to a strange and different world. However, the travel is not accomplished using a spaceship, or by surpassing the speed of light; you simply close your eyes, lie back, and away you go.

This technology is not yet perfect. The time and place that you arrive cannot be chosen and is rarely the same. You can't predict what peculiar persons you may encounter on your journey, some familiar and some quite novel. This kind of travel is all the rage. Many travelers enjoy it *because* it is unpredictable, strange and marvelous, because your actions and adventures in this alternate world have very few consequences to deal with. This unpredictability comes with a price: some trips are frightening. People don't seem to mind this much. Some even like it.

Dream Travel

This science-fiction scenario should seem familiar. It's just like ordinary dreaming. This could be what happens when we go to sleep. In Neil Gaiman's *The Sandman*, it happens on a regular basis: people travel back and forth between the waking world and the Dreamworld. Could our dreams really be trips to such a place?

There are many specific features of Gaiman's Dreaming, Dreamscape, or Dreamworld, as it is variously called, that our dreams might not have: they might not be influenced by the rule of Morpheus, and the world we visit might not contain Cain and Abel's constant feud. After his escape in *Preludes and Nocturnes*, Morpheus travels to the waking world (but it doesn't seem to be by sleeping, or by waking for that matter). So there's more than one way to get to the Dreamworld in *The Sandman*, but there may be only one way to get to our dream world, the dream world in reality.

Leaving these specific details aside, could our dreams be travels to a place that really exists? Could a fantastic dreamy world like Morpheus's exist, and do we effortlessly travel there whenever we dream?

Butterfly Dreams

The idea might seem a little crazy at first. You have probably heard sayings like the one originating with the Chinese philosopher Chuang Tzu (Chuang Chou) after he dreamed he was a butterfly:

> Once I Chuang Chou, dreamed that I was a butterfly and was happy as a butterfly. . . . Suddenly I awoke, and there I was, visibly Chou. I do not know whether it was Chou dreaming that he was a butterfly or the butterfly dreaming that it was Chou. ("The Equality of Things," *A Source Book in Chinese Philosophy*, p. 190)

Thinking along these lines leads you to start wondering whether you can trust the evidence of your senses. When I'm dreaming I usually don't know it. So when I believe I've woken up, what I take to be sights and sounds revealing the real world may be fleeting illusions. I may be dreaming. This kind of worry can also be found in western philosophy as early as the Greek philosophers Plato and Aristotle.

But this concern is a little different from the question we're considering here. We might be a little worried by Chuang Tzu's thought, but it's not enough to convince us. People don't seriously think that their daily experiences are butterfly dreams while their nightly dreams are reality (whether butterfly realities or some other kind—not everyone is lucky enough to dream of being a butterfly).

We might take something else from Chuang Tzu's question: maybe the point is just that there really isn't a huge difference between dream and reality, so we can't really say which is which. That's an interesting idea too, but also not a convincing one. After all, dreams are weird. Morpheus's dreamscape is also weird, featuring living fables, talking ravens, and things blinking in and out of existence.

Our question is whether the weird experiences that happen in our dreams could be experiences of an objectively real place, a place that exists somewhere outside of our heads. When we think of the world where our waking lives unfold, we think that most of it is there, and will continue to be there, whether we and our minds are there or not. It doesn't *depend* on our minds. It's mind-independent. Some things are obviously mind-independent: rocks, trees, and other people. Other things are obviously not mind independent: my belief that Morpheus is one of the Endless. The existence of that belief depends on me, specifically my mind and what it thinks. So can our weird dreams be experiences of a place that is mind-independent?

I'm assuming the default answer here is going to be "no," or possibly, "No. *Sandman* is a good story, but I think maybe you should see a doctor." Dreams are supposed to be random sparks from neurons, inspired by recent experiences and perhaps serving some greater purpose, like memory formation, and they are supposed to be completely subjective or mind-dependent. Something like that seems to be the consensus these days.

It's not completely clear whether dreams in general are mind-independent in *The Sandman*. Consider when Morpheus summons the Hecateae to tell him the location of his lost tools. He seems to gather bits of dreams from different people and to bring them together: "the crossroads comes from a Cambodian farmer. . . . the black she-lamb is more difficult, but one DANCES in the dreams of a child in ADELAIDE, Australia . . ." (*The Sandman: Preludes and Nocturnes*, p. 71).

Here it seems as if what dreams there are, what building blocks Morpheus has to work with, depends on individual people's psychology. Of course, these specific elements may be drawn from the dream world into people's dreams, whence Morpheus retrieves them. In contrast, there are specific elements of the Dreamworld, such as Lucien and Morpheus's castle, that have been there for ages and clearly don't depend on any single human mind for their existence.

Dream things may depend on Morpheus's mind. The integrity of the Dreamworld seems to depend to some extent on Morpheus. Lucien, Morpheus's groundskeeper, says, "You are the incarnation of the dreamtime Lord. And with you gone, the place began to decay, began to crumble . . ." (pp. 67–68). Lucien goes on to describe how words disappeared from books and certain creatures simply vanished. But many things remained in his absence, though decayed and weakened. Morpheus says, "The DREAMWORLD, the DREAMTIME, . . . call it what you WILL—is as much part of ME as I am part of IT" (p. 71).

This kind of dependence on the creator may be consistent with the mind independence we are interested in. Many famous philosophers have believed that God upholds the existence of our world in one way or another. I think we can safely say that there are some aspects of the Dreamworld that are at least as independent of minds as ordinary reality. Some things in ordinary waking reality, like people's beliefs, depend on minds. For all we know, everything depends on God. Let's say that what we are interested in is whether actual dreams could be at least as mind-independent as ordinary waking reality.

The Idealist philosopher George Berkeley noticed that all perceived qualities, primary ones like shape and motion in addition to secondary ones like color and temperature, are in some sense mind-dependent. This suggested to him that there is no need to assume an external world in addition to peoples' experiences. Sights and sounds and feels do not give us evidence of real objects: the sights and sounds and feels are all there is to the objects; there's nothing else.

However, this leaves one unresolved problem: how is it that our subjective experiences are ordered, that different people see the same things at the same times, and that when we return after a coffee break, things are, more or less, as we expect? Berkeley said this was possible because God kept experiences ordered to create uniformity in our perceptions. For all we know Berkeley's theory could be true of the waking world. Furthermore, while dreams may not be as ordered as the waking world, whatever order they have may be upheld by Morpheus in the same way that God upholds the appearances in the actual world according to Berkeley.

This idea makes sense, and it is not just a philosophers' idea: many cultures and religions believe or have believed that dreams are objective in this sense, that a place like Gaiman's Dreamworld exists. So why are we, now, so confident that it doesn't? Why are we so sure that our dreams are fleeting, subjective, in some sense less real than our waking life?

I Dream Therefore I Am

Like Chuang Tzu, René Descartes, in his *Meditations on First Philosophy*, allowed himself to doubt his sense experiences, partly because they are like dreams. Descartes was moved by the thought that he could conceive of any waking experience happening in a dream and remaining convincing. Furthermore, in dreams we suffer illusions—there are not actually external objects corresponding to our experiences. Descartes reasons that there may not be objects corresponding to waking experience either.

In the end Descartes decides there is an external world (that's a relief, I'm sure). Our waking experiences are different from dreams. For one thing dreams lack the continuity of our waking life. Memory can unite the episodes of our waking life, but fails to connect dreams with one another or with the whole course of our lives. Dreams are, largely, detached episodes.

This lack of continuity threatens the objectivity of dreams, too. If dreams are just as objective as waking life, why do they seem so episodic? Recall the super-technological travel scenario I described at the start of this chapter. In that scenario, we never know where, or when, we will arrive. This is a limitation of the travel technology, and perhaps the same can be said for our sleep travel. In that case, it is not surprising that the events of sleep are discontinuous: there is no coherent narrative for memory to construct from these disparate travels. Of course, sometimes we encounter people from the past, or have dreams that repeat, and memory is able to keep track of those.

The dream travel scenario is what philosophers call a thought experiment. A thought experiment is like a regular experiment, but without all the beakers and stuff. We just think of a scenario and see what follows from it. Here we confirmed that there is at least one scenario where the discontinuous nature of dreams is consistent with the objectivity of the dream world. Unless we have a reason to rule out that scenario, we shouldn't conclude that dreams are not objective simply because they are discontinuous.

If we are unmoved by Descartes's continuity argument, then his conclusion that there are objects corresponding to our waking perceptions should apply equally to dreams. A lack of continuity does not prove a lack of objectivity, and many other considerations in favor of objectivity seem as compelling for dreams as for the waking world.

Descartes suggests that we should consult all of our senses, memory, and understanding and check that they are in agreement to test the accuracy of our experiences. He thinks that when we know the origin, time, and location of a perception, we can be confident we are awake. Maybe so, but that still doesn't give us a reason to doubt the mind-independence or the objectivity of dreams.

Another threat to the objectivity of dreams is that things ebb in and out of existence in dreams: a friend or maybe Morpheus himself appears then disappears. Our thought experiment can be adjusted to account for this too. One possibility is that the travel machine is a little glitchy and we are jumping to other locations mid-dream. However, this only accounts for complete changes of scene. It does not explain one item disappearing, or one person morphing into another, like Judy Garland into the Wicked Witch and Aunt Em in Hal's dream (*The Sandman: The Doll's House*, p. 186).

These kinds of changes can be explained too, by assuming that the natural laws governing the Dreamworld are different from those governing the ordinary world. Worlds with these kinds of laws seem possible. In fact, some of the actual laws governing the waking world as detailed by quantum physics seem equally bizarre: non-locality, the uncertainty principle, superposition of states.

This might start to seem like a stretch, but dreams, like the quantum world, are strange, and I don't think the possibility of dreams being governed by different laws can be immediately excluded. After all, we're assuming that, like the Dreamworld, dreams are an objective world very different from our waking world. On the other hand, this suggests a bigger problem with the objectivity of dreams.

It Was and It Wasn't

YOU'RE DREAMING. ANYTHING'S POSSIBLE.

—Unity Kinkaid, *Doll's House*

Perhaps our doubts about the objectivity of dreams arise because dreams are often inconsistent, fleeting, sometimes even blatantly *contradictory*, and the objective world is not. We have all found ourselves honestly describing our dreams by saying: "It was Dave, but it also wasn't Dave—you know what I mean?" But there can be no contradictory states of affairs. There is nothing that both is and is not my can of deodorant spray. This seems to be the most severe critique that can be made against the mind-independence of dreams. The argument is simple:

There are contradictory experiences in dreams.

There are no contradictory objective states of affairs.

Dreams are not experiences of objective states of affairs

If we can refute this argument, that would get rid of a big obstacle to the mind-independence of dreams. It would at least be possible that dreams are mind-independent, that they are objective.

There are different strengths of possibility. In a dream we may soar effortlessly and unassisted across the sky, or stand casually atop a pristine lake. These events contradict the laws of physics in our world. They are physically impossible. Yet we can imagine a world with different laws of physics where these things are possible. We are interested in a stronger grade of possibility, logical possibility. If we dream of some single thing that both is and is not Dave, at the same time, we're dreaming of a state of affairs that is logically impossible. A sentence describing this state of affairs must be false because it says that the very same thing both is and is not the case, but according to classical logic, exactly one of those claims is true. Dave is either there or not.

Dreaming is a kind of mental activity, as is perceiving or thinking or imagining. Like these other activities, dreaming of something implies that we conceive of it. This gives the dream of a contradictory state of affairs a kind of existence, but not yet objective existence. The philosopher Alexius Meinong became well known for claiming that when we think about certain fantastical objects, like Morpheus's pouch of sand, we are thinking about something, so that thing (not just the thought) must exist in some way. He called the kind of existence had by fantastical objects (and some other kinds of objects) subsistence. Bertrand Russell replied to Meinong with an analysis of the structure of sentences and thoughts involving non-existent objects. When we think, "Morpheus has a pouch of sand", the structure of our thought is:

> There exists something such that that thing is a pouch of magic dream sand, and there exists something else such that it is the unique King of the Dreamworld, and the first thing has the second thing.

There are a few things to notice about that sentence:

1. It is ridiculously silly.

2. It looks better in logical notation:

$\exists x \exists y\ ((((\mathbf{S}\mathbf{x}\ \&\ Ky)\ \&\ (\ x \neq y\ ))\ \&\ Bxy)\ \&\ \forall \mathbf{z}\ (\mathbf{K}\mathbf{z} \rightarrow (\mathbf{z} = \mathbf{y})).$

See! Much better.

And **3. the sentence is a claim about the existence of things satisfying certain descriptions.**

If those things don't exist the sentence is false. This doesn't require commitment to the existence of any fantastical objects. We are not thinking about the pouch, we are thinking that there exists a pouch with magical sand, but there doesn't (probably).

Unlike Meinong I don't argue directly to the conclusion that non-existent objects, or in my case contradictory states of affairs, exist (or subsist). I simply say that we conceive of them. Russell's reply does not contest that; it simply specifies a way that we conceive of them.

There is a kind of argument that concludes from the fact that something is conceivable, that it is possible. For example, David Chalmers argues in his book *The Conscious Mind* and elsewhere that philosophical zombies are conceivable, so they are possible. A philosophical zombie is a being that is physically identical to an actual person but that lacks conscious experience. If philosophical zombies are possible, then it seems that there is more to being conscious than having certain physical characteristics.

Similarly, we might argue that because we conceive of logically contradictory states of affairs, those states of affairs are logically possible. The trouble is that "conceive" here is shorthand for something like entertain, imagine, think about, or what-have-you, without contradiction. It might seem that we can't think about a contradiction without contradiction; that when we conceive of a proposition and its denial it is apparent that at least one must be false. But in dreams it seems that we conceive of a contradictory state of affairs without contradiction: we have an experience and thought about something that both is and is not Dave, and there is no experience or sense of contradiction, no need to reject either claim.

But can there really be contradictory states of affairs corresponding to these experiences? Could it ever possibly be true that this person is Dave and that this person is not Dave? Contradictory states of affairs don't seem imaginable, and that is the view traditionally taken by philosophers, but recently some philosophers such as Graham Priest have seriously defended the view known as dialetheism, that some sentences are both true and false.

Let's just say that dreams may present us with the objects that make sentences both true and false, and make dialetheism true. The person seen in the dream both is and is not Dave. Since it is possible to conceive of contradictions, then if we do experience contradictions in dreams, we're not forced to conclude that dream experiences are not real.

If we experience a logical contradiction in a dream, for example a person who both is and is not the Dream King, then it is conceived and conceivable. A state of affairs in which both a proposition and its denial are true is held before the mind. If it is conceivable, then it is logically possible. At least on certain views of truth like dialetheism, these states of affairs are logically possible; conceivability even of a contradiction implies possibility. If true contradictory statements and contradictory states of affairs are possible, then conceivability is probably a good indication that a state of affairs is possible (though failure of conceivability may not be a good indication that it is not possible).

This means that these contradictory states of affairs could obtain, or could have obtained, in the actual world. It's possible, though very unlikely (except perhaps in quantum physics), for contradictory states of affairs to exist in the waking world. However, in the Dreamworld and in dreams, the likelihood of the objective existence of contradictory states of affairs is much greater.

Dazed and Confused

The alternative to contradictions being possible is that we don't conceive of contradictions in dreams, at least not clearly. Perhaps we only seem to. These experiences are confused. That is part of what made Descartes's considerations about dreams so compelling: we can be convinced that any waking experience might be a dream experience partly because we know our judgment in dreams is clouded. Maybe our judgment is clouded when we seem to have contradictory experiences. But if we only seem to conceive of contradictions in dreams, we cannot conclude that contradictory states of affairs are possible.

If this is right, then there's no longer an obvious problem for us to explain. If the appearance of contradiction in dreams is illusory, then it doesn't imply contradictory states of affairs and doesn't count against the existence of an objective dream world. Not all dream experiences are contradictory, and the ones that seem to be contradictory may have been wrongly interpreted.

This conclusion is consistent with dreams being, by and large, experiences of an objective, mind-independent world. After all, we form confused judgments and perceptions in waking life quite often. There is a long tradition of philosophers arguing from the fact that experiences are sometimes illusory to the conclusion that they always are. Whatever such arguments may be worth, dreaming and waking life are on a par with respect to objectivity.

Our strongest reasons for not believing in an objective, mind-independent dream world have been dispelled. A place like the Dreamworld could exist and our dreams could be travels to such a place. Given that we have dream experiences every day and they are sometimes very convincing, we also have good evidence that there is such a place.

6
Apologizing to a Rat

JONAS-SÉBASTIEN BEAUDRY

As I wrote this very paragraph, I was sitting in a café close to Union Square in New York. When I got out of the subway, I asked three people: "Which way is North?", before someone looked at me. The others walked past me and I felt insulted. Though I did eventually find North and my way out of that café, I was startled to realize that invisibility is everywhere and—ironically—easy to see.

All of us have treated people as though they were invisible and we all have been treated as though we were invisible. Not all invisibilities are as extreme as the one metaphorically presented in *Neverwhere*, however, there are degrees of invisibility and degrees of its wrongness. Invisibility can be radical and correspond to a complete exclusion from the moral community. In that sense, one can think of slaves in societies which allowed for slavery, or of Jews in Nazi Germany as invisible peoples. Although there is a huge difference in terms of wrongness between ignoring a beggar in the street and committing a state-orchestrated genocide, both events involve dehumanization and indifference which can be understood in terms of misrecognition of needs and lack of moral standing.

Neverwhere, Neil Gaiman's first and his own personal favorite novel, explores these questions of morality and invisibility. *Neverwhere* is a paradigm of the "urban fantasy" genre as it tells the story of characters evolving in a "magic city," a "London below," which is characterized by an archaic, semi-anarchic, semi-feudal political structure of clans, suzerains and mercenaries. It is inhabited by a melting pot of humanoid creatures and animal-like humans, including vampires, rat-speakers, angels, monster-like villains, and magically gifted humans. Their social interactions are regulated by tribal allegiances and mercantilism. Some characters belong to "noble" families, others survive miserably, begging and bartering.

The geography and characters of this magical world are a parody of London, more particularly, of its subway system. Some of its characters are allegories for London locations and underground stations: the "Old Bailey," the central criminal court in London, becomes an old bird-like man, "Earl's Court," a London neighborhood and subway station, is a senile earl surrounded by his minions, including a jester(!), "Serpentine," actually a minor tributary of the Thames, is the leader of Amazon-like warriors).

The story takes the form of a quest, in which the hero, Richard Mayhew, an ostentatiously ordinary chap, helps Door, a character from London Below, to escape evil mercenaries sent after her. As a result of his involvement in the world of London below, Richard becomes invisible in his own world: he loses his fiancée, his job and the capacity to be perceived altogether. He sets out to find Door in London below for help. Although his initial quest is to go back to things as they were before he met Door, he will ultimately help Door rather than himself and, although he finally regains visibility in his own world, he decides to go back to live in London below.

The theme of invisibility is central to the story as it is the curse that Richard tries to lift all along. The project of *Neverwhere*, initially a TV series, started with a BBC producer asking Gaiman to write on "tribes of homeless people in London" (interview with Gaiman in the Harper Perennial edition of *Neverwhere*). Readers may be familiar with the mediatized reality of homeless people living in underground train stations and we certainly know how the poor and the homeless are socially ostracized and ignored.

If someone is invisible, we don't notice them and therefore we don't consider them worthy of moral consideration. We don't think about whether we should help a person if that person does not even appear on our moral radar screen. Whatever system of morality we favor, whether it is to maximize happiness or to do what Jesus would do, the outcome will be vastly different according to which persons or entities we notice as being worthy of moral consideration.

We're faced with moral demands from all sides every day and there are many socially condoned or even recommended strategies to avoid the demands that strangers or people from our own community or friends make upon us. Our indifference to the needs of others can be less extreme than that of a slave-owner for a slave. Certain people and entities could also simply fall low on our scale of priority. As Hannah Arendt famously said, evil is banal and can be the result of a failure to relate properly to people who suffer: it does not take uniquely evil masterminds and exceptional circumstances for aloofness to prevail. That is not to say that indifference or ignoring some-one else's needs is always necessarily bad, but only that it is a common phenomenon.

How to Be Invisible

Neil Gaiman's creation of an alternative magical world which coexists with ours is a perceptive critique of the indifference between social classes and between larger communities. A good starting point for our analysis of invisibility is to describe the sort of invisibility that afflicts the hero, as he becomes part of this almost invisible world populated with almost invisible characters.

Gaiman's magical invisibility can also be only partial, and, as such, it resembles real-life indifference, which is never quite so radical as to render human beings literally invisible. People can perceive Richard if they pay close attention to him, just as we could perceive an extra in a movie if we paid close attention, but people hardly notice him. Their attention "slid off Richard, like water on an oiled duck"(p. 59).

His office space is being emptied, his work colleagues hardly perceive his presence; when he insists, they do not recognize him and ask him who he is. His ex-fiancée, who broke up with him after he decided to help Door, does not recognize him. Potential tenants visit his apartment that has been put on the market and do not notice that he is in the bath. His invisibility is therefore variable, as it is sometimes partial and sometimes complete, as when he calls the police and the person at the end of the line cannot hear him.

These consequences may be magical in *Neverwhere*, but they all sound sadly familiar. Compare Richard's inability to take possession of his apartment with the limitations on ownership placed on specific groups in particular historical circumstances. As our identity is partly constituted by social recognition, the exclusion of a person from his work, family and social environment can very well make him "invisible" by taking away his various social roles: that of a company employee, a work colleague, a friend, or a husband. Consider how easily people from a higher social class may fail to mingle with those from a lower one and simply ignore the poor and the homeless. People may also ignore other beings because they belong, not to another social class, but to another race, religion, or gender. Lawrence Blum cites an incident where a taxi driver ignores a Black woman and her child, to pick up a white male instead.

Jews, Muslims, homosexuals, women, slaves, indigenous people have all been denied the privileges granted to full members of the community that they seemed to inhabit. They were excluded from the moral community, a community of members who give each other an equal core of respect. They could not access the same public services, buy at the same shops, ride the same public transport, attend the same schools, or enjoy the same civil rights.

What is being denied in such cases is not only a list of particular rights or benefits but the status of a being who can, in theory, receive such rights and benefits. Richard is very happy when a taxi stops for him at the end of the story: "a cab stopped for him—it stopped!—for him!". The cause of his joy is obviously not the possibility to have a cab ride, but to have gotten back his visibility, his status as a person whom other moral agents must consider, a rights-holder, a full member of his moral community, someone whose claims we must give some weight to.

Seeing Invisibility

The most obvious way of being invisible is to be physically invisible. *Neverwhere* is not the first story about unnoticeable people who actually become transparent. In these stories, physical invisibility is generally used as a metaphor for real-life invisibility which does not necessarily affect the being physically, but only some dimensions of his identity which are not acknowledged or recognized. Gary, Richard's co-worker, does not recognize Richard, but is still polite toward him, in a way that he would not be toward a rock or a completely invisible being.

Oddly enough, we are good at compartmentalizing our ignorance of others. When I ask a colleague "how are you?" without caring much about the answer, I am certainly acknowledging his role as a co-worker in this office, his right to a form of polite acknowledgement of his presence. I am relatively unconcerned, however, with his well-being or his needs in general. Concern is most often partial, rather than complete or non-existent. That sort of invisibility is better understood as applying to particular aspects of a being rather than to the being as a whole.

However, Richard's plight reveals that invisibility is not always partial. When the moral worth of a being is completely ignored, invisibility affects not only certain needs, traits or roles of a being, but the being as a whole. Such a being is radically excluded from our community and is not to be morally taken into account at all. Understanding the phenomena of "total invisibility" requires us to question why the possession of certain properties, such as being rational, being Christian, being white or being part of "London above," is a necessary condition for belonging to our moral community.

Invisi-*where?*

I see Richard's passage from London above to London below not just as the passage from one community to another in the ordinary sense of a community, but as an exclusion from the moral community. A moral community is a community of beings entitled to moral consideration. Outsiders become morally worthless, like rocks, and may be used to achieve our ends. They have not only become unimportant, but they have also lost their very statuses as human subjects and they have no value of their own in the eyes of moral agents. They are morally invisible.

We belong to many micro-communities, of culture or of interests, at the same time. Geographically, Richard works in a specific office and lives in a particular city. Socially, he has colleagues, a circle of friends and a fiancée. The role we occupy, as co-worker, fiancé and friend, imposes particular duties on us, as well as on others toward us. As Richard becomes invisible, these reciprocal duties disappear. His former friend and his former fiancée certainly had duties to help him, but they no longer recognize him: they are merely polite to him and they do not consider that they owe him more than some basic token respect. His phone and his bank cards no longer work, cab drivers will not stop for him, subway employees will not sell him tickets, and no one will notice that he's stuck in the train door when it starts moving.

Richard has not become totally invisible. He has become invisible to some people. This is why invisibility in *Neverwhere* should be discussed in a concrete and in a relational way. Richard has simultaneously become invisible to the inhabitants of London and visible to the inhabitants of London below. The inhabitants of London are not invisible to the inhabitants of London below, but this visibility is only formal. The folks populating London below may well be aware of the inhabitants of London above, but they do not care about them: it's as though they can't be threatened by them and can't threaten them either. This is the ideal representation of completely independent societies. They are so hermetically separated that their members cannot belong to both at once.

Why, then, did Richard make such a transfer to London below? How do we lose our visibility, our status as a being worthy of consideration?

Ways of Becoming Invisible

There are two ways in which we can explain how Richard and other characters become visible or invisible in *Neverwhere*; they correspond to the absolute or partial sorts of invisibility. Someone is made completely invisible when they are considered as falling outside of our moral community altogether. But someone becomes partially invisible when they fall outside of our relations and life plans, are not involved in our dramas, are neither an ally nor an enemy, and have not developed any closeness to us.

How did Richard make a transition to London below? It happened because he performed a benevolent action toward a person belonging to London below. That and other actions make him visible to some people from this strange society, as he becomes the subject of threats from underworld creatures which had previously ignored him, and eventually invisible to the inhabitants of his previous world with whom he loses all ties. Being a Good Samaritan may not pay off when your concern is directed at someone outside your community.

It's easy to compare Richard's misfortune with real-life cases in which doing the "right thing" can alienate us from our community. Consider the social cost of being friendly with someone unpopular at work or of freeing your slaves in a slave-owning society, or the repercussions of hiding Jewish people under the Nazi regime.

Richard's passage to the other world is illustrated by a ritual. He follows instructions to go to an imaginary address; these instructions take him to some narrow, almost invisible streets in which he turns counter-clockwise thrice, which clearly marks some sort of magical ritual. In real life, although rituals may aim at changing the nature of reality, like dancing to provoke rain, or performing certain actions in order to become a werewolf, they most commonly serve a myriad of non-magical social functions. Rules of etiquette serve as a useful moral landmark for daily social interactions with strangers; the solemnity of various forms of legal agreement serves to make certain of the consent of the parties concerned; procedural fairness contributes to legitimize various branches of the State's exercise of authority. Typically, the more complex or grave the rituals, the more radical and irreversible the effect. The particular effect here is the passage from one community to another. Again, such an effect is not purely fictitious. There are rituals for converting to a religion or becoming a citizen of a nation.

Richard also meets people from the underground community with whom he creates a variety of relationships, further reinforcing his belonging to the new community. Once he has become radically invisible in London above, Richard cannot go back to his old world unless he lives marginally, like the two homeless characters living like sub-humans in-between worlds, Iliaster and Lear. The Marquis de Carabas tells Richard that "it isn't a good life" (p. 340), because it would deprive him of the satisfaction of the fundamental need for social recognition and sociability.

Important elements constituting the narrative of Richard's life have been transferred to a different community. The creation of ties and personal attachments or the sharing of values and interests with members of that new community have made him invisible to the people of his former community. Some communities are mutually exclusive and some are not. For instance, being part of a community of moral vegetarians is incompatible with being a member of mass-production meat farming industry, but not with being a Presbyterian.

Gaiman's fantasy is thus grounded in real human reactions. If you sit with a row of homeless people on the sidewalk and speak with them kindly and with empathy, they may well reject you at first, indeed, the first reaction of the "rat-speakers" to whom the beggars bring Richard is to want to kill Richard, but they eventually come to help him, just like the beggars may accept you. When you look up to people walking on the sidewalk, you will find that your relation with them has changed. You may be much less visible or audible to them.

Humanity Unseen

When we say that someone is dehumanized, we mean that they are not treated with the minimal respect owed to all human beings. Dehumanizing treatments may be inflicted upon a person for many reasons, such as cruelty, hatred or self-interest, but it could also be, as Richard Rorty noted, that the torturer, the rapist and the murderer simply fail to recognize that they are dealing with a "real" human. When a being is dehumanized, they are construed as being external to our moral community. They can make no claim on us, we do not have to take their interests into consideration, we won't even bother to reflect upon their needs and how we could meet them.

In *Neverwhere*, Jessica completely excludes Door from her moral horizon. She doesn't consider her well-being at all. She keeps walking, dragging Richard along, when Door falls into their world through a door which has magically appeared in front of them. Door steps out, sways, and collapses on the concrete. Only Richard can see Door. "He could not believe" that Jessica was "simply ignoring the figure at their feet." Richard's own nature as a fellow human becomes tainted as he meets people from London below.

The most straightforward way to operate a radical exclusion is to simply decide that a group, like all Black people, immigrants, or animals, is not worth taking into consideration at all. This is difficult to justify because these beings undeniably have needs and a fate of their own that begs to be respected. It's not obvious why we should fight against our gut feeling that we should at least take their well-being in consideration to some degree when we deal with them. One way to exclude them is therefore to misconstrue these needs. Jessica says of Door, who is bleeding to death, that "She just needs to sleep it off," as though she were a drunk passed out in the street. In practice, this misrecognition of someone's real needs can have the same effect as depriving them of moral standing.

Indifferently Invisible

We saw that a radical way to ignore the moral demands that others can make on us is to construe these others as beings who are not entitled to make such demands upon us. They fall outside of the realm of beings who we will consider morally. This requires some clear rule to demarcate the frontiers of our moral community. People who are only concerned with the worth of their fellow citizens, or people of a certain religion or a certain color, use such a standard. Another more moderate way to ignore the moral demands of others is by limiting conceptually the demands that they are entitled to make. They will not be completely invisible, they will still be rights-holders and we will still acknowledge that they have needs and that they are owed duties, but just "not by us". The relation we have with these beings is such that we are obligated to them only in some limited regards.

For instance, Door will become visible to Jessica because Richard will make her see that Door exists. Then, Jessica will misconstrue Door's needs, but Richard will also make her see that Door truly suffers. Then Jessica, having properly acknowledged Door's existence and needs, will deny that whatever duties is owed to Door is weighing on her shoulders: "We're going to be late. Someone else will come along; someone else will help her." And then, compromising, "Dial 999 and call an ambulance. Quickly, now. . . . When you call the ambulance, . . . don't give your name. You might have to make a statement or something, and then we'd be late"(pp. 24–25).

Jessica is only respecting one of Door's most basic rights: her right to life. And even that basic respect, she concedes unwillingly. Could this indifference be morally justifiable? If we think about the situation in an abstract way, it seems justified: moral agents do not owe very stringent duties to strangers. Calling for an ambulance is enough, carrying Door in one's arms to one's house seems morally noble, but not morally obligatory. Yet, is this abstract view capturing all that there is to moral obligations? Richard's obligation to help Door cannot really be accounted for from an impartial and abstract moral point of view.

Avoiding Invisibility

So Jessica and Richard react very differently to Door's first appearance in London above. Having seen someone in pain and in need of help, "Richard shivered and stopped in his tracks", while Jessica "tugged him into motion", simply stepping over the crumpled form and "ignoring the figure at their feet" (p. 24). Jessica and Richard have not categorized Door in the same way and they are not looking at her with the same sort of attentiveness.

Why the different responses between Richard and Jessica? An inclination for compassion, for a "loving gaze," as Iris Murdoch would say. This notion has been interpreted to mean an "intuitive openness which involves feeling rather than thinking, and a quietness which reduces distracting background noise or racket." Such "noise" includes other considerations, like our desires and agendas, which may influence us to distort relevant facts about people, such as their needs. Jessica's preoccupations, for instance, help to explain her indifference.

How is the moral agent to adopt this loving gaze? By giving a "just and careful attention to an object which confronts her." Once Richard has adopted this attitude and is confronted with the suffering of Door, he cannot escape his duty. The ethical obligation seems to be the result of an intuition, rather than a process of logical reasoning. Richard's epiphany happens when he is summoned by Door's "face" and pays a "just and careful attention" to her:

> Suddenly the girl's eyes opened, white and wide in a face that was little more than a smudge of dust and blood. "Not a hospital, please.

They'll find me. Take me somewhere safe. Please." Her voice was weak. "You're bleeding', said Richard, . . . Why not a hospital?" "Help me?" the girl whispered, and her eyes closed. (pp. 24–25)

And so Richard "picked the girl up, cradling her in his arms" and took her to his place. Jessica threatens him to put an end to their engagement if he walks away. But the obligation weighing on Richard comes before any possible rationalization about what is owed to whom and about whether it is sufficient, from an impartial point of view, for a diligent citizen to call an ambulance and walk away. "Richard felt the sticky warmth of blood soaking into his shirt. Sometimes, he realized, there is nothing you can do"(p. 25). There is nothing he can do because he cannot intellectualize, or abstract, himself away from his duty, which comes prior to thinking "Richard did not, at any point on his walk, stop to think."

Some philosophers have pointed out that this kind of approach to moral obligations is messy. What if Door hadn't looked at him, whispering "Help me?", would he still have helped her? Maybe Door's plea and fragile state can better explain Richard's psychological motivations than justify his moral obligations.

The answer to such a criticism is that Richard does not react in an attentive, concerned way, for morally irrelevant reasons—or instance, because he finds Door pretty, or because she reminds him of someone he liked, or of himself. Gaiman makes it clear that Richard hasn't at first realized her sex, under the dirty, bloody rags. He helps Door because he is a virtuous person and is well aware of his own flaws. By contrast, Jessica is not very self-aware. She doesn't know that her selfish and ambitious tendencies make it likely that her way of looking at Door will mischaracterize her in order to rationalize her behavior and give herself a good conscience.

A sort of practical wisdom allows Richard to balance Door's and Jessica's needs properly. Richard may well stand in a much closer relation to Jessica, his fiancée, than to Door, a stranger, and most of us would think that it would be the appropriate thing for him to do to help Jessica instead of Door. Most of us think that if Door and Jessica had the same need, having their lives saved, Richard should save his fiancée. But most of us would not think that all of Jessica's desires, like her need not to be late to her appointment, should trump Door's, her need to live, given the gravity of their respective needs.

It would be acceptable for Jessica, on her way to her meeting, to refuse to listen to a stranger who wanted to tell her about his political views. She would be slightly undermining that stranger's well-being, but the nature of the relation she has with him does not impose the obligation to listen to him, even though she might know that allowing that stranger to share his political view with fellow citizens like herself would contribute to his well-being. It's not acceptable, on the other hand, to let someone, including a stranger, die in order not to arrive five minutes late to a meeting.

But—Jessica could answer—I will not only be five minutes late. I will miss this meeting, look bad with my boss, fail to obtain this promotion which is very important to my sense of self-realization, my goals and aspirations, what matters to me. We live in a society which is much too big for me to personally take care of the needy. My ignorance is not explained by a lack of moral character—I wouldn't expect anyone to pick me up if I fell down. This is why the State exists. I pay taxes so that ambulance drivers take care of these strangers who are making incessant demands on me, that I must ignore in order to have time to achieve something meaningful with my life.

This explanation would interpret social invisibility as the result of social atomization, but it is no less a failure to interpret the sort of needs, community and relationships we are dealing with. Jessica's justifications for helping or refusing to help someone else is based on the idea that only a certain type of moral obligation is really mandatory—those social rules to which she has agreed for her own benefit. Reciprocity of concern being fundamentally based on self-interest, this sort of justification allows for a community which breeds habits of indifference, of quick rationalization to dismiss the moral demands that others make on us.

This way of thinking selfishly, rather than being natural, rather seems like a rationalizing spell that one throws on one's own moral intuitions. After all, Jessica is able to recognize the sort of duties and community that Richard is referring to when he tells her that they must stop to help a person who is hurt. We're tempted to say that the fact that she recognizes this sort of duty immediately and with little explanations reveals that

Richard is pointing out to her some moral truth or at least something that is appealing to her in some ethical sense. Jessica's quick reframing of Door's status as a drunk homeless who only needs to sleep rather than a suffering stranger in dire need of help also reveals that she is denying something. Now, we've seen Jessica's answer: this something is not ethical, it is psychological weakness, a sentimentality bearing no moral consequences. Richard has no sense of priorities, she says to herself. This is a good example of how abstract and impartial moral reasoning may fail to capture the whole of our moral obligations.

Richard himself wonders if what he has done has any sense once he starts reflecting upon his action. For, as he takes Door home, in spite of Jessica's threat to break off their engagement if he did, "Somewhere in the sensible part of his head, some-one—a normal, sensible Richard Mayhew—was telling him how ridiculous he was being: that he should just have called the police, or an ambulance; . . . that he was going to have to sleep on the sofa tonight; that he was ruining his only really good suit; that the girl smelled terrible." At this point Richard is borrowing Jessica's moral view of the situation.

Once Jessica has put all strangers in a same category, it becomes easier to excuse herself for not helping Door. It seems arbitrary to help Door to the degree Richard helps her, as he carries her in his arms to sleep in his home, because she is afraid to go to the hospital, if one does not make reference to the fact that fate put Door across Richard's path and that Richard decided to seriously take on the role of Good Samaritan.

Apology Accepted

It is a compassionate, loving gaze upon Door which made her visible to Richard. Such attention to living beings around us may allow us to question whether we should help a being to whom we are normally indifferent or that we normally catego-rize as morally negligible. This concern may allow us to over-come our ignorance of that being's particularities. The knowledge that we acquire may help us to challenge the social misconstructions of the nature and needs of traditionally mar-ginalized groups. We may discover that the homeless don't always just need to sleep it off, that Black people and women are not naturally less intellectually gifted, or that a rat is something to be treated with courtesy.

The moral of the story is that invisibility is a widespread phenomenon that we should combat, first by acknowledging the needs of invisible people, and then by doing something about these needs. Addressing needs, the novel promises, will make us better people. Richard asks Door, "You want me to apologize . . . to a rat?" (p. 42). Because Richard will apologize, more to humor Door more than anything else, this rat will later save his life. In London below, where different social norms govern and rats are highly noble creatures, the rat will no longer be invisible to Richard as a moral entity. Because he will help Door, instead of looking away, and sacrifice his engagement with Jessica, he will become a fuller, happier person.

At the end of the novel, Richard leaves, maybe we should say transcends, the real world to go live in the magical London below, which evokes the blessing of an afterlife (p. 370). In real life, not only are we generally too weak to attend the needy, but we are often only too happy to opportunistically let them stagnate in their invisibility, so that we can hide from our moral weakness. But Richard is a hero and heroes are noble creatures imagined to show us the way and support our intuition that being moral is worth sacrificing some of our self-interest.[1]

---

[1] This chapter is dedicated to my brother.

7
Seeing Isn't Believing

KANDACE LYTLE

Have you ever considered the possibility that someone created this world in order to entertain you? Distract you? Possess you?

Most people assume the world we exist in is one that should be accepted as is. Why question it, right? This is the very conundrum the young heroine of *Coraline* must grapple with when she encounters the sinister other world behind the door in the drawing room. Though this new world appears delightful at first, Coraline quickly discovers there is more to it than meets the eye. If she's to survive, Coraline must decide what to trust: her senses or her reason.

René Descartes was a philosopher interested in whether or not the world we interpret with our senses is a world we should believe to be real. He explores the possibility that the external world may have been created by an evil genius. According to Descartes, an evil genius might be trying to deceive us into a false sense of comfort by producing a world devised to entrance and seduce us.

Like Descartes, Gaiman's gutsy girl Coraline questions the portal world she enters through the door in the drawing room and seeks to find out why it has been created. She must venture into the world of an evil genius—the other mother—dismiss her senses and use her intellect to both conquer the evil genius and remove herself from a world created to entertain, seduce, deceive, and possess her.

See You on the Other Side

Coraline is considered children's portal fiction—fiction where magical doorways or portals connect two locations that are separated temporally or spatially.

In children's portal fiction, specific locations serve as thresholds between two worlds: the real and the fantastic. The protagonists in children's portal fiction find themselves transported from their own world to another world; often those worlds are parallel worlds, past or future worlds, or spiritual places like heaven, purgatory, or hell. Like Frank Baum's Oz, J.M. Barrie's Neverland, Maurice Sendak's world of the Wild Things, and Lewis Carroll's Wonderland, the world Neil Gaiman's Coraline discovers is an alternate universe that imitates and duplicates her own world making this new world— the other mother's world—a realm of fragmentation and disintegration.

The other mother's world blends the boundaries between the authentic and the fantastic—or, in this case, the uncanny, because the other mother's world is something familiar, yet different in a discomforting way. Coraline must negotiate where and how she fits in both worlds; her ability to conquer and make sense of the flexible nature of the other mother's world gives Coraline power and authority, enabling her to discover a sense of self and belonging she lacks at the beginning of the story.

Although Gaiman borrows familiar conventions of portal fiction—*Coraline* is often likened to *Alice in Wonderland*—he revises the traditional portal by adding persons and animals who are neither quite here nor quite there: Coraline's feline friend who lacks a name and often a body; ghost children trapped behind a mirror, basically in purgatory; Coraline's other mother who is able to manipulate the space, objects, and people within the other world; and even Coraline (as Karen Coats puts it) is in a "transitional state, a state where . . . she is developing a separate sense of self" from her parents and trying to understand who she is because her own sense of self has been disrupted by a recent move to a place where no one knows her name or tries to understand her.

Gaiman's incorporation of this portal world and the ambiguous figures within it allows Coraline's own world to be subverted, causing Coraline to seek to find the "I" within Coraline.

Do My Eyes Deceive Me?

Sometimes we awake from a dream, and wonder whether or not it actually occurred. Because of the in-between space we inhabit both inside and outside of our minds while dreaming, Descartes is skeptical about the state of humans while they're dreaming; it is often dreaming that leads many characters in portal fiction to the in-between spaces.

In his *Meditations on First Philosophy*, Descartes begins by recognizing that he has often been mistaken about claims he once believed to be true. In response to this, Descartes offers a rationalist theory, in which a person interprets the world around them by focusing on the mind guided by reason and the intellect, rather than relying on the senses to acquire knowledge. Descartes believes that our senses can deceive us. He feels that although dreams seem real, dreams cannot provide persons with knowledge. Having rejected the senses as reliable sources of knowledge, Descartes comes to the question, "How do I know if I'm awake or if I'm dreaming?"

Often readers of children's literature ask this question of their favorite protagonists. All of the alternate worlds mentioned above—Oz, Neverland, Wonderland, and the world of the Wild Things—come to fruition once Dorothy, Wendy, Alice, and Max have fallen asleep, yet Coraline's other mother's world proves to be an exception to this. Rather than falling asleep before entering the other world, Coraline must be left alone.

Once Coraline is alone, she encounters the world of the other mother or, to use Descartes's terminology, the world of the evil genius. Because Coraline is awake when she discovers the world of the evil genius, Gaiman sidesteps Descartes's skepticism about the dream world. When Coraline first moves to her new house, she discovers a small door in the drawing room and out of curiosity asks her mother for the key.

When Coraline and her mother open the door, it simply opens to a wall of bricks. Later, Coraline's mother goes to the grocery store, leaving the inquisitive child alone to entertain herself. Coraline unlocks the door once again, only this time it leads to another world. Gaiman plays with the traditional convention of children falling asleep before they are able to explore a fantastic world. Rather than forcing the reader to believe the other mother's world is one Coraline can only encounter in dreams, he shows the reader that the other mother's world is one that exists parallel to Coraline's world. Gaiman does not leave the reader to question whether or not Coraline is dreaming, but forces the reader to accept the fact that Coraline has entered a portal world through the door in the drawing room.

Gaiman plays with the idea of dreaming in relation to the other world again later, once Coraline returns from her first trip to the other mother's world. Coraline finds that her parents have gone missing. She hopes that by falling asleep, she will awaken from a horrible dream filled with creepy other mothers and fathers with button eyes to find herself in her own world and her real parents restored. Instead, Coraline finds her parents have actually been kidnapped by the other mother and she must enter the other world once again in order to save them. Coraline must venture into this other world in order to better understand herself outside of the world that surrounds her; her parents must leave her alone in order for her to discover the other mother's world.

Like Descartes, she enters a world devised by the evil genius, one she must doubt completely in order to better understand who she truly is. Unlike Descartes who begins his meditation asking whether or not he is dreaming, Coraline knows she is awake; she accepts the uncanny nature of her situation: "She knew where she was: she was in her own home. She hadn't left. . . . A woman stood in the kitchen with her back to Coraline. She looked a little like Coraline's mother. Only, . . . only her skin was white as paper." Coraline knows this other world actually exists and believes she must enter it prepared to encounter a world created to deceive her, a world created by the other mother, or as Descartes would call her—an evil genius.

Smoke Gets in Your Eyes

Descartes's evil genius is an evil god-like entity who deceives people into believing false things by manipulating the world around them. Descartes never explains the evil genius's motivation for deceiving humankind, but maintains that if we doubt the everyday world of solid objects, which is what the evil genius is able to manipulate, then truth lies in our ability to think. We must doubt our sensory perceptions because they are not the source of true knowledge.

Gaiman's other mother character is able to manipulate the world around Coraline as well, but Gaiman gives his character motivation—the other mother hopes to possess a child of her own. When Coraline first encounters the other mother, she does not initially believe her to be an evil force. Like the evil genius, Coraline's other mother is a being able to manipulate the world around her so as to mislead Coraline and all those who enter the other world into believing that untrue things are true. However, as Coraline moves through the other mother's world, she discovers that the other mother is more evil and selfish than she had suspected at first.

Coraline recognizes the other mother's world as a duplicate of her own home—only something is slightly off, but she can't quite place her finger on it. Coraline's other mother lures her in with a plateful of delicious food—who doesn't love perfectly cooked chicken and potatoes?—and then leads her to the kind of room that every child dreams of: the other mother has created a beautiful bedroom with interactive toys and allows Coraline to play with cute, friendly little rats.

As Coraline continues to move through the other mother's world, she finds that her neighbors in this world are much more entertaining and interesting than they are in her own world. Mr. Bobo's rats can speak and have actually mastered their circus act, and both Ms. Forcible and Ms. Spink perform for Coraline and an audience of enthusiastic Scottish terriers who love chocolate—Warning: your Scottie might not be as enthusiastic as those in the other mother's world, after swallowing the first few pieces.

This adoration and the attention the other mother and Coraline's neighbors give Coraline is amplified in the 2009 movie version of *Coraline*. At the end of the film, Coraline's desire for material objects and attention is still very present; whereas, at the conclusion of the novella, Coraline is more self-sufficient and relies on her intellectual abilities to develop a strong sense of self, rather than depending on the corporeal world and other individuals to define her.

The movie enables the viewer to experience how sensational and alluring the other mother's world truly is. The other mother's dinner table is no ordinary dinner table. When Coraline's other mother suggests the addition of gravy, a little choo choo train—a literal gravy train—circles the table and dumps a load of gravy upon her plate. In addition to the over-whelming display of food Coraline encounters at the dinner table, the film version of *Coraline* contains an adoring other father who uses Coraline as his muse to write songs and to create a beautiful garden in the shape of Coraline's face. The other father in the movie is a carefree soul with a jazzy, upbeat swing, which is a serious improvement on Coraline's real father, who has neither the time nor the energy for her. As the movie continues, the viewers learn that the other father has been created by the other mother; therefore, the other mother furthers her relationship with Coraline in the film version by creating a bond between Coraline and the other father as well.

All of the experiences Coraline has in the other mother's world appeal to her senses—delicious food, beautiful gardens, entertaining neighbors who put on elaborate shows—which is what Descartes believes we should be most skeptical of. Descartes asserts that the world of the senses leads to decep-tion. He believes that the external world is a world of disillu-sionment; one that tempts us with alluring sights, sounds, smells, tastes, and physical sensations. The other mother's world is created to appeal to Coraline's sensory experience of the world.

Coraline comes to recognize that all that she has consumed with her eyes, nose, tongue, ears, and body are undesirable things manipulated into pleasant experiences by the other mother. Like Descartes's evil genius, Coraline's other mother manipulates that which surrounds her in order to deceive Coraline: "The other mother could not create. She could only transform, and twist, and change" (p. 124).

All of the tasty food and friendly neighbors Coraline encounters in the other mother's world have been transformed by the other mother to persuade Coraline to stay with her. The encounters the other mother facilitates between Coraline and her neighbors cause Coraline to feel accepted by the commu-nity that surrounds her, a situation that has not occurred in her own world where everyone calls her Caroline instead of Coraline. In the real world, Coraline's neighbors and parents deny her existence and do not give her the necessary attention a bored and lonely child needs; yet, in the other mother's world, Coraline feels her identity is confirmed and that she is being supported by her other mother and father and her neighbors.

The other mother's ability to seduce Coraline by using the external world illustrates Descartes's belief that as a being living in a world created by the evil genius, it's tempting to give in to the seductive nature of the senses. Just as the other mother's world is not truly Coraline's home, according to Descartes, the world we experience with our senses is not the true world.

In Descartes's Second Meditation, he examines the malleability of a piece of wax. Descartes uses all of his senses to observe the wax in flux and witness the changes the wax undergoes as it moves from a solid to a liquid once it is heated by a fire. When he places the wax near the fire, he observes that although the wax melts the same piece of wax remains. Descartes wonders how we come to the conclusion that the solid piece of wax and melted piece of wax are the same substance. He asserts that our understanding of the solid and melted wax is not derived from the senses, since the wax's properties change in the melting process. Therefore, Descartes asks where else his understanding of the melted wax and solid wax as the same substance comes from.

He dismisses the senses as a primary form of understanding because all of the sensible qualities of the wax change after the wax is melted. He understands that true understanding cannot come from the imagination, for if he imagined the wax, it would be able to change into an infinite number of shapes and sizes. Instead, Descartes believes that the intellect alone must be the answer; he believes his mental perception of the wax might be confused by the senses or the imagination, yet, his perception of the wax is clear if he practices a careful mental analysis of the wax using his intellect alone. Like Descartes's evil genius, Coraline's other mother prompts Coraline to rely on her intellect alone, for if she relied on the senses and imagination, Coraline would be trapped by the seductive nature of the other mother's world.

The other mother's desire to seduce comes from her desire to capture Coraline to make her stay in the world she has created forever. Gaiman's creation of the other mother gives us a different interpretation of Descartes's philosophy. It highlights the fallible nature of the senses, but also points to how easily it is for humans to err in their perception of the world around them. Descartes's wax example illustrates how humans can be taken in by the senses, but Gaiman pushes this further in the other mother's world by having the other mother give Coraline everything she could possibly desire. In doing so, the other mother's deception becomes manipulative seduction, which is never a motive attributed to the evil genius.

Not Seeing Eye to Eye

Whether reading the novella or watching the movie, we see that the other mother hopes to fulfill Coraline's every wish. But Coraline decides to leave the other mother's world when asked to sew buttons in place of her eyes. What would occur, exactly, if Coraline accepted the offer? Coraline replacing her eyes with buttons may seemingly be a cosmetic change, one that only results in a change in appearance. Yet could this exchanging of eyes represent more? Could it represent Coraline's loss of autonomy?

Descartes explains that if we surrender to the evil genius we lose our autonomy. Our autonomy is what allows us to make choices for ourselves; if we give in to the false world the evil genius has created for us, then we're placing our perceptions over our self-directed activity. The hazard of losing our autonomy is one reason why Descartes believes we should not trust our senses. Replacing her real eyes with buttons would mean that Coraline was rejecting the real world because the other mother's world was more gratifying.

If Coraline replaces her real eyes with buttons, will she still be the same person? Coraline suspects that replacing her eyes with buttons might somehow alter her ability to make choices for herself. All of the other people and creatures in the other mother's world have button eyes; so perhaps if Coraline decided to sew buttons in place of her eyes she would be sacrificing her free will and independence.

By asking Coraline to sew buttons in place of her eyes, the other mother is trying to establish a deeper connection with Coraline, so we can deduce that both the possibility of returning to the real world and the loss of autonomy could occur if Coraline made such a sacrifice. Until she is asked to make a sacrifice in order to stay in the other mother's world, Coraline simply recognizes the positive qualities of the world the other mother has created. When the other mother makes this creepy request, Coraline senses danger and decides to leave; she refuses the other mother's offer and returns home to find her parents have been kidnapped by the other mother.

When Coraline returns to the other mother's world, she immediately asks the other mother where her parents are, to which the other mother replies, "Whatever would I have done with your old parents? If they have left you, Coraline, it must be because they became bored of you, or tired. Now, I will never become bored of you, and I will never abandon you. You will always be safe here with me." Coraline accuses the other mother of lying, so the other mother touches a nearby mirror and presents Coraline with a video-like look at her parents claiming they are happy without her.

By disregarding the other mother's explanation for her parents leaving she illustrates Descartes's argument that people must question the reality created for them by others, specifically by the evil genius. Coraline's rejection of the other mother's explanation for the absence of her parents causes the other mother to become irate and push her into a mirror where she finds three ghost children whose souls have already been devoured by the other mother. These soul-less bodies illustrate the gravity of the other mother's power to possess Coraline, for they have lost their autonomy and memories.

Later, as Coraline moves through the other mother's world attempting to free the ghost children and her parents, she begins to understand that the other mother created the world not only to fulfill all of Coraline's desires, but to fulfill her own selfish wish to possess a child. When the other mother pushes Coraline into the mirror, Coraline is disturbed by the ghost children's inability to recall their lives before they were captured by the other mother. The children tell her that "names are the first thing to go" and that they have kept their "memories longer than their names." This disenchantment with names and preference for memories reinforces Descartes's theory that the corporeal world and the names associated with the objects in it are not as important as our own ability to understand ourselves by using our minds. Coraline's journey throughout the other mother's world serves to assure Coraline that people mispronouncing her name is not as important as Coraline knowing who she is.

Aside from the ghost children, one of the characters who helps Coraline discover herself by using the method of

Cartesian doubt is the nameless cat. Once she has escaped the mirror, Coraline has become quite the little Cartesian and one of the characters who has helped lead her there is the nameless cat who does not possess a double in the other mother's world and is able to move freely between the two worlds, as Coraline does. In Coraline's first conversation with the cat, he criticizes Coraline for assuming that an "other" cat exists: "I'm not the other anything. I'm me. . . . You people are spread all over the place. Cats, on the other hand, keep ourselves together. If you see what I mean."

As Coraline pursues her quest to find her parents and release the souls of the three ghost children, her conversation and reliance upon the cat illustrates the need to know ourselves in order to succeed in a world where our senses can deceive us. By forming a relationship with a creature that understands the danger of the other mother's world, Coraline is able to decipher the difference between appearance and reality. The cat's guidance and support allow Coraline to change from a being who relies on others to help her understand herself and make decisions to a person who values her autonomy and understands the importance of free will.

On a Clear Day You Can See Forever

Unlike Coraline, who is bothered by others mispronouncing her name, the cat feels that names are not necessary; in fact, he asserts that the naming of people and things is done in the absence of true self-knowledge in order to allow those objects and people to know what and who they are. "Now, you people have names. That's because you don't know who you are. We know who we are, so we don't need names."

Like Descartes, the cat recognizes that the only thing that you need to trust is yourself. The cat knows who he is; therefore, he is. He does not need a label nor does he need to be recognized by other beings; he simply exists outside of that which surrounds him. This makes him more powerful than Coraline because, as Descartes points out, in order to overcome the evil genius, you must be able to trust your own thoughts—*Cogito ergo sum*, "I think, therefore I am." Throughout the course of the novella, Coraline is striving to uncover this truth; for once she understands that knowledge and belief in herself is necessary for her to thrive in both the other mother's world and her own, she is able to become independent.

Throughout the novella, Coraline is constantly trying to define herself in relation to the people who surround her. She becomes frustrated when her neighbors mispronounce her name, after all Coraline is more unique than Caroline. She pleads with her mother to purchase her DayGlo gloves in order to set herself apart from all of the other uniform-wearing children at her new school: "But Mum, *everybody* at school's got gray blouses and everything. *Nobody's* got green gloves. I could be the only one." Coraline becomes an independent person child who doesn't need recognition from others in order to feel important.

At the beginning of the novella Gaiman offers the G.K. Chesterton quotation: "Fairy tales are more than true: not because they tell us that dragons exist, but because they tell us that dragons can be beaten." Coraline's defeat of the other mother gives her self-confidence, so much so that before beginning a new school Coraline is not "apprehensive and nervous" as she usually is the night before the first day of term. Instead "there was nothing left about school that could scare her." Coraline doesn't need DayGlo gloves to feel ready for school. She has become independent from her parents.

At the end of the movie, by contrast with the book, Coraline is still very much the same bratty and needy child she was at the beginning—unfortunately, the film version does not do Coraline justice; it simply turns her into a spoiled brat, rather than portraying her as Gaiman does, as a bored and lonely child with whom we sympathize. The movie Coraline relies on the addition of a male character, Wybie, to aid her in conquering the other mother, and still desires to be in the company of those who have ignored her by organizing a garden party. Another disappointment is that the end of the movie delivers a message similar to that of Sendak's *Where the Wild Things Are*—our parents will love us no matter how impossible we are. Coraline is given the DayGlo gloves, just as Max discovers a piece of cake left for him at the end of *Where the Wild Things Are*. Coraline is still relying on others to face her fears.

The desire for recognition Coraline possesses at the end of the film is not one of Coraline's main concerns by the end of the novella, in which Coraline does not ask her parents to acknowledge the fact that she saved them from the other mother, nor does she allow her neighbors to mispronounce her name; at the end of the novella, she aggressively corrects Mr. Bobo after leaving the other mother's world. Coraline's reliance upon herself as a source of truth and power illustrates Descartes's belief that the mind is more important than sensory experience because it guides us in our endeavors.

Like Lewis Carroll's Alice, Coraline encounters a world where the seeking of comfort from that which surrounds her becomes both impossible and, in itself, discomforting. Alice experiences a world where madness is embraced and no one will provide her with answers—much like the world Descartes hoped to dismiss in order to better understand what types of knowledge can be discovered using reason alone. Coraline experiences a world where the appearance of a seeming reality is created by the other mother, a manifestation of Descartes's evil genius.

Unlike Alice, a girl who only questions the madness of the world surrounding her, and is not seeking to find truths about her own existence by questioning herself, Coraline discovers that possessing a true understanding of herself is necessary in order to fully exist.

After defeating the other mother, Coraline understand that the other mother's desire to possess someone who has self-actualized stems from her reliance on the flexible nature of the physical world. By the end of the novella, Coraline discovers who she is, just as Descartes uncovered absolute truths about self-existence.

Coraline's inability to identify with or trust the world around her reflects Descartes's struggle against empiricism: by surrounding ourselves with a world of objects, animals, and humans whose existence must be doubted, Cartesian thought and Coraline's quest both prove that the 'other' world is one in which we always exist, whether or not we enter it through a portal.

Coraline is able to find the "I" in Coraline, just as Descartes was able to uncover the importance of the *cogito*, by questioning the evidence of her senses and using her mind to attain independence.

The Grim Teacher

8
The High Cost of Learning

ANDREW TERJESEN

One day in every century, death takes on mortal flesh, better to comprehend what the lives she takes must feel like, to taste the bitter tang of mortality. And this is the price she must pay for being the divider of the living from all that has gone before, all that must come after.

—*Death: The High Cost of Living*, #3

That's the story they tell in the world of Neil Gaiman's *Sandman*. The idea of Death becoming mortal is not a new one. Most notably it's the basis for the 1934 film *Death Takes a Holiday* and the 1998 remake *Meet Joe Black*. But in both of those films Death makes a one-time decision to walk among humans and does so out of curiosity. Gaiman's Death becomes mortal once every hundred years and the activity is seen as an important part of making sure she does her job well. But why? And how does this teach Death anything?

We eventually learn that Death did not always spend one day as a mortal every hundred years. She chose to do so after a simple encounter. As Death explains it, "One day a small girl looked at me when I took her, all icy and distant and vain, and she said, 'How would you like it?' That was all she said, but it hurt me and it made me think" (*Vertigo: Winter's Edge*, #2). It's pretty clear that the impetus for Death's mortal sojourn is the perception that she lacks any compassion for those she collects as she dies. And the girl's challenge reflects a commonly-held belief, that the best way to develop compassion for someone is to spend some time in their shoes.

Like a lot of common sense and conventional wisdom this just seems obvious and we don't give much thought to it. But it actually raises philosophical questions. Why isn't it enough to be told that people are afraid to die? Why does she have to think about how it would make her feel in order to understand? Why wouldn't imagining that she's mortal be just as effective as actually experiencing mortality for herself? And what is it about mortality that cannot be conveyed in words or even in abstract ideas?

The Sunny Side of Death

When we first meet Death in the pages of *Sandman* (Issue 8 to be precise), she does not appear at all as one might expect. Her demeanor is almost the exact opposite of what one would expect from someone who spends all their time ushering people into the next life. And it's certainly a stark contrast with her dour, morose brother Dream. Upon meeting her (though not quite aware of who she is yet), Hob Gadling calls her "Little Miss Sunshine" (*Sandman,* #73).

In her second appearance, we see an even softer side to Death when she takes time out of her busy schedule to talk to the despondent Urania Blackwell. Death shows up telling Urania, "You just looked like you might need someone to talk to" (*Sandman*, #20). Ironically, Urania is trying to find a way to die, but Death can't help her because she has been transformed into a near immortal being by the Egyptian God Ra. Her fate is dependent upon Ra's whims, as Death eventually explains to her. In talking to Urania, we learn a lot about Death's attitude towards her job. According to Death, "I'm not blessed, or merciful. It's just me. I've got a job to do and I do it." Gaiman has said that he intended Death's cheery sense of responsibility to be a contrast with the reluctant attitude of Dream in carrying out his duties.

Death wasn't always so warm and positive. In a story that takes place long before the events of the *Sandman* series, Death enters a room stating, "I was invited. I have come. Make of that what you will. . . . I am making you uncomfortable. I shall leave. Decide what you like at your parliament. It is all one to me. It won't make a lot of difference, in the long run, will it? One by one, you will all come to me" (*Sandman: Endless*

Nights). This is a far cry from the Death who checks in on Urania. What's even more disturbing is that she's addressing a parliament of stars and universes, but her demeanor is such that it makes these celestial bodies nervous. Death does give us some insight into what was running through her head at that time. As she explains,

> A really long time ago, I used to think I had the hardest job in all of my family. It was fine at the beginning. At the very beginning, dying and living were new things and people did them with the enthusiasm they always bring to new things....After a bit, it got harder. The only people who greeted me with relief did so as an escape from something bad or intolerable. The rest of them just wished I'd go away, as if dying were some kind of admission of failure. It made me sad. (*Vertigo: Winter's Edge*, #2)

At one point, things got so bad that she just stopped acting like Death. Once she had seen the consequences of a world without death, she went back to work though she was still bitter and sad. She didn't need to experience mortality in order to see how important death is for a smoothly functioning universe. She looked at the results of her inaction and realized that she needed to go back to doing her job. But knowing that it was an important job didn't make her any happier about doing her job.

Death underwent a major transformation in attitude only much later and she attributes it to her mortal-one-day-every-hundred-years program. But the why is still not very clear. What did she learn as a mortal that she could not have deduced as a member of the Endless? After all, Death means the end of one form of existence and uncertainty about what the next one holds. Why did Death have to experience it for herself in order to appreciate how scary that is for people? It seems like one could figure that out based on what people were saying when they met her. The little girl's response that inspired the mortal-one-day-a-century shtick seems to indicate a great deal of frustration with life having ended so soon.

Life and Death Aren't Black and White

If Death had to experience mortality in order to experience her change in attitude, then that means that there was something she learned through the experience that could not be conveyed through any other method. Not every truth needs to be conveyed through experience. Based upon the physical properties of human bodies, I know that I couldn't survive a fall from a mile in the air. I don't need to experience it first-hand. Similarly, I understand the nature of infinity even though by definition my finite mind could not experience infinity as infinity. On the other hand, the only way we can understand what it's really like to see something blue or taste something salty is to actually do these things. To know what it's like to have a sensory experience you just have to have that sensory experience.

In her day on Earth as Didi, Death experiences a lot of the little sensations that make up a mortal existence. At one point, she remarks, "Don't apples taste great? I mean the way they taste and the texture. And the way when you chew them they kind of crunch and the juice runs out in your mouth. Isn't it amazing?" (*Death: The High Cost of Living,* #1). Sure, she describes some of the aspects of eating an apple by referring to its "kind of crunch" and the juice running out, but these words seem more to gesture towards our memory of the experience than they actually describe the full content of the experience. It seems as if our memories have to do some of the fleshing out for us to understand what Didi is saying.

So, it is possible that what being mortal teaches Death is what it feels like to be alive—to breathe, to eat, to love, to be afraid, and all the other sorts of experiences that one would not expect an anthropomorphic personification to have. This still doesn't tell us why such sensory experiences are so important in changing Death's perspective. But before we try and answer that question, it would be a good idea to re-examine our core assumption—that we can't understand what it's like to see the color green without actually seeing the color green.

The philosopher Frank Jackson presents an interesting hypothetical scenario to test this assumption.[1] He asks us to imagine a color scientist named Mary. Mary has been living her whole life in a black and white world. It's not that she can't see

---

[1] Jackson introduced this thought experiment (usually known as "Mary's Room") in his article "Epiphenomenal Qualia" and expanded upon it in "What Mary Didn't Know."

color, it's just that she has been locked in a room with only black and white objects her whole life. Her only access to the outside world is through black and white television signals. During this time, she has learned everything there is to know about the physics of color vision—how the angstrom of light waves correspond to different colors, the process by which these light waves trigger a response in the rods and cones of the human eye, how the signal is transmitted through the optic nerve to the visual system, and so on. The important thing for this thought experiment is that she not only knows everything we currently know about color vision, but she also knows everything that science will ever be able to tell us about color vision. After she has learned everything she can possibly know about color, she is finally freed from here prison and walks out into the world where she encounters a red rose. The question is, when she finally sees the rose, does she learn anything new about seeing the color red?

At first, the answer to this question might seem pretty obvious. Look at what Didi says about hot dogs: "Is the chemical aftertaste the reason why people eat hot dogs? Or is it some kind of bonus?" (*Death: The High Cost of Living*, #2). Anyone who has eaten a hot dog understands what she's referring to, but imagine trying to describe that taste to someone who's never eaten a hot dog.

However, in answering that way, we might be focusing too much on our ability to describe it in everyday language. If we knew more about the composition of hot dogs (though who would want to spoil the surprise?) and the way that our taste buds worked, we might be able to convey to someone the nature of the taste. What Mary the color scientist is really asking us to consider is whether we think there are certain things that can only be understood from a first-person perspective.

The particular impetus for Jackson's hypothetical example was to challenge us to think about whether science (which involves third-person explanations) could ever fully explain our subjective experiences (since they inherently involve a first-person perspective). Will science ever be able to bridge the gap between the impersonal phenomena of the universe like our neurons and the personal phenomena of our thoughts? This is a slightly different question than what we're concerned with, but it boils down to the same problem—can someone ever understand what it's like to be a different kind of being with a different way of experiencing the world?

As in all thought experiments, there's no indisputable answer to Mary the color scientist. Some people are convinced that Mary must learn something new when she sees red and others are just as committed to the opposite conclusion. What both sides need to do is present good reasons for their particular view. The real challenge for those who want to argue that you really need to taste a hot dog in order to know what a hot dog tastes like is that science has been getting better and better at explaining what was once thought to be inexplicable.

To rule out the possibility that science could one day enable us to "read" people's experiences off of their brain functions, we need to identify something that necessarily defies scientific explanation. This isn't easy. The most obvious choice would be to identify something about experience that is non-physical, a sort of soul or mind that rides on top of our brain. However, that opens up a big can of worms because we now need to explain how it is that a non-physical system can interact with a physical one. So, even if it is theoretically possible that all aspects of life could be described in a third-person way, it would be a fairly impractical method for conveying the information. Didi and Sexton (the young man who, ironically, befriends Death after a failed suicide attempt) have the following exchange:

> **SEXTON:** You like being locked up in warehouses and being threatened by loonies, and…
>
> **DIDI:** No. I didn't like that. But . . . it's part of the whole thing. And there is a whole thing out there. And it's all part of living. The good bits and the bad bits and the dull bits and the painful bits. (*Death: The High Cost of Living*, #3)

There are a lot of things to living, and it would be hard to list them all off the top of your head. Instead of describing all the possible aspects of your experience, it would be much easier to simply run a simulation. Admittedly, one life is not going to capture all there is to living, but that's okay because Death becomes mortal more than once. So, it turns out, we don't need to claim that there's something we can only learn by experience. It's enough to point out that some things are just much easier to learn through a simulation than by merely hearing them described. A particular individual could learn how to pilot a plane by reading all the right books, but more people would learn (and at a faster pace) by practicing it after some instruction.

Death in a Mortal Coil

A wide-awake reader might point out that the example of Mary the color scientist doesn't truly represent the situation that we're trying to understand. Mary the color scientist is someone with the capacity for color vision who just hasn't had a color experience yet, though she has had plenty of experiences of seeing things. It's not so strange to think that she might be able to connect the facts about color that she has learned with her experiences of black and white vision in order to understand a color experience before she actually has one. But Death trying to understand mortality is more like a blind person trying to understand sight or a human trying to understand how a bat sees the world.[2] Didi tells Mad Hettie, "I'm no one special today" but the experiences Didi has seem to belie that claim (*Death: The High Cost of Living*, #1).

Throughout her day with Sexton she makes comments which show that she knows that she is Death and that the mortality thing is only for the day. She tells Sexton that the people in the picture really aren't her parents, "That's just the universe's way of making me feel more comfortable. Technically right now I'm about three hours old." The fact that she's well aware that she's a construction enabling Death to experience mortality indicates that Didi is not really experiencing the world as normal people do. Sexton thinks she's crazy, because those are the kinds of things a crazy person would think.

The fact that Didi knows what is going on presents two concerns for her ability to really understand what it is like to be mortal. To begin with, she knows that she's going to die and that she has only one day to experience life. While some people may feel that way, it's unusual to have the kind of certainty that Didi must have (since we never see her questioning her

---

[2] The famous article which began many of these philosophical discussions is "What Is It Like to Be a Bat?" by Thomas Nagel.

own sanity). Didi does not live with the uncertainty of life. This is only a problem though if the lesson she needs to learn is connected with life's uncertainties and humanity's fear of death. I'll argue later that this is not the case—at least in the *Sandman* universe.

A second and greater concern represents what I like to call the "Soul Man" Effect. The name comes from the first place I encountered this idea, the under-appreciated C. Thomas Howell classic *Soul Man*. In that 1986 movie, Howell plays a character who's so desperate to get into Harvard Law School that he pretends to be African American in order to get a scholarship. As happens in all 1980s identity-bending comedies, the deception is eventually exposed and Howell's character has to spend the last half-hour of the film demonstrating that he learned something through his experiences by making appropriate restitution to those he has wronged. One of the last scenes involves him talking to the imperious professor played by James Earl Jones, who remarks that Howell must now have some understanding of what is to be Black in America. Without missing a beat (and of course showing how much he had really learned), Howell's character says that he hadn't really learned anything because he could always have stopped his deception and therefore stopped being African American. Didi would also experience the Soul Man Effect because she knows that when she "dies" she'll go back to being Death.

In addition to the Soul Man Effect, there are lots of other ways that Didi's experiences are unusual. As Sexton notes, she never seems to pay for anything (*Death: The High Cost of Living*, #2). Didi started the day with exactly the amount of money she needed to get through the day—ten dollars to buy a new ankh (the symbol of her status as the mortal embodiment of Death) and two pennies to pay her way into the next life. In the course of her adventures with Sexton, she also encounters various supernatural beings like the Eremite and Mad Hettie. Again, not something that happens to the everyday person even in the *Sandman* universe. To be fair, Didi's understanding of what she is seems to fade as she gets closer to her death, so she might not be experiencing the Soul Man Effect at the time of her death.

Whether the Soul Man Effect is relevant depends on what it is that Death needs to learn. In the case of race relations, one really needs to understand what it is like to be judged according to something that is an inextricable part of you. In the case of mortality, it might not be necessary to experience all the things we associate with death. Didi's knowledge makes her cocky, as she admits when she and Sexton are trapped by the Eremite. Perhaps that's a mistake she needs to make and learn from. Once we figure out what exactly it is that Death learned that caused her transformation in personality, we should be able to determine what parts of mortal existence need to be included in Death's one-day existence.

What Has Death Learned?

According to Death, here's how her first day of mortality ended:

> After the first day I was alive, when I met me, I turned to me and I told me I was a cold-hearted, stuck-up, frigid bitch. Only I didn't say it anywhere as nicely. And I got the message. You see, when someone's died, mostly they're a bit shaken, or hurt, or angry, or worse. And all they need is a kind word, and a friendly face. (*Vertigo: Winter's Edge*, #2)

The main lesson that Death learned was that she needed to comfort those who'd just passed on—but does that really require such an elaborate lesson plan? By Death's own admission, the lesson she learned wasn't exactly deep, but it still took her a while to learn. During that confession, she describes her realization in the following way:

> At the end, each of us stands naked. At the end, each of us stands alone.

This way of putting it is philosophically deeper than the idea that everyone needs to see a smiling face at the end. It harks back to some existentialist philosophers who claim that death is the one experience we can't share with anyone else. Since death is the end of one person's life, no other person can share in that (since it would be their end instead).

Once again, it's not entirely clear that this is a lesson that requires direct experience. The existential philosophers who have argued for this idea have done so from a 'logical' perspective and their conclusions have persuaded people who were themselves a long way from dying. And this particular lesson is complicated for Death as the peculiar nature of her one-a-day existence interferes with the idea that Didi "stands alone" when she dies. The consciousness Didi has of being a part of Death undermines her ability to experience that particular lesson for herself. However, this points us to another possible lesson Death might learn from her experiences as a mortal. And much like the existential lesson, it is related to helping her understand why people are in such need of comfort when they die.

In Death's second mini-series she's a more marginal character as the focus is shifted to human characters Foxglove and Hazel (who first appeared in the *Sandman* series). In the course of that series, Death helps Hazel to understand the "meaning of life." Death tells Hazel, "If you're going to be human, then there are a whole load of things that come with it. Eyes, a heart, days and life. It's the moments that illuminate it, though. The times you don't see when you're having them . . . they make the rest of it matter" (*Death: Time of Your Life* #3).

Admittedly, Didi was quite focused on life's little pleasures and did not seem to exhibit the human tendency towards distraction that causes us to often miss life's little moments. But Didi represents an incarnation of Death who has largely learned her lesson, so one would expect Death to make the most of life when she lives it. Hazel sums up Death's lesson as follows, "Mostly we're too busy living to stop and notice we're alive. But that sometimes we do. And that that makes the rest of it matter." This sounds like the kind of lesson that could only be learned when you're immersed in the distractions of life, alongside other people who are equally overwhelmed by living. Even Death's peculiar existence would contain episodes where she would be tempted to lose sight of the little moments and this makes her very aware of the distractions that living beings face in their pursuit to stay alive.

What humans often forget—at least until they meet Death—is that a lifetime is all anybody is promised and a lifetime is not a specified length of time. While it's important to plan for things like retirement, we should not put all our energy into a future that might not come. We need to be sure while we're preparing for tomorrow that we take time to enjoy today. And since there is no specific amount of time that we should spend on the "little moments," it is very likely that people, when they first realize they are dead, begin to think of all the times they should have had little moments. Death would learn first-hand what it feels like to have that realization.

Death's ability to comfort the recently dead—the enormous change in attitude that she had after a while of engaging in the mortal-one-day-a-century program—comes out of this understanding of why people feel the way they do upon dying. In her early days, Death was probably ticked off that people wouldn't just quickly accept their new reality and move on. But as Didi tells Sexton, "If you know someone really well it's hard to be mad at them for very long. . . . I know everybody really well" (*Death: The High Cost of Living*, #2). Death's experiences as a mortal gave her insights into a particular aspect of the experience of living that could not be readily conveyed to an immortal. How do you explain to someone the tension between trying to live for today and worrying about tomorrow? How can you convey how easily someone can get distracted from the things which are most important? Presumably anyone who grasps Hazel's epiphany does so because they can think of a time when they didn't stop and smell the roses and how they regretted it afterwards.

Why Isn't the Lesson Over?

At one point in her earthly existence, Didi comments, "I love food. Food is so great. I mean, it's so much more fun than photosynthesis . . . or having a power pack in your back, or bathing in liquid crystals, or any of those things. . . . I've been doing this one-day-a-century bit for quite a long time now" (*Death: The High Cost of Living*, #3). This tells us two important things, Death has been doing this for a while, and she has not been limiting herself to the human experience in her explorations of mortality. The fact that she experiences all sorts of mortality is probably an indication of the fact that different existences have different distractions and different ways of dealing with them. If Death is to be able to comfort all deceased creatures, she needs to be aware of any possible idiosyncracies that might shape their response to being dead. Even if it were possible to explain all the differences to an omniscient being, living it is probably a faster way to simulate all the possibilities. But why does she need to keep doing it, now that she seems to have learned her lesson?

The answer can be found in the very nature of the lesson. People have a mixture of emotions when they die, because dying makes them realize what was really meaningful in life. It probably leads them to worry that they did not enjoy enough of the "little moments" while they were alive and makes them want a little more time so that they can go back and savor what they missed. Death needs to live a mortal existence so that she can understand why so many people can lose sight of the "meaning of life." But that lesson needs to be reinforced. If Death were to stop experiencing mortality, she might slowly forget the experiences that are key to appreciating this point. She runs the risk of once again becoming the gruff immortal whose attitude is "You had your time, it's your fault for not making the most of it" (especially when there are a fair number of cultural sources that try to remind us of that lesson).

Again, Death seems to have learned the importance of the little things (like the taste of a hot dog). But her one-day-a-century existence can still reinforce the overall lesson. Didi's last words are "No, please, I—" (*Death: The High Cost of Living*, #3). This shows that even though she knows that she isn't really going to cease to be and that she has enjoyed the little moments, she can still feel like there isn't enough time to "truly live." After Didi's death, Death talks to herself (in the form of Didi) and this is their exchange:

DEATH: How was it?

DIDI: Oh, it was wonderful. It was filled with people. I got to breathe and eat and . . . all sorts of stuff. I wish it could have gone on forever. . . . I wish it didn't have to end like that. . . .

DEATH: It always ends. That's what gives it value. When you get to be alive, even for a day . . . Well, there's only one way to stop living. Was it worth it?

DIDI: I . . . I don't know. I think so. I hope so. I met such neat people. . . . I wish it could have gone on forever.

Didi's conversation with Death must be for the reader's benefit. The sum total of Didi's experiences from that day with

Sexton have to be conveyed to Death directly in some manner in order for this to be a meaningful exercise. If the short exchange was all that was necessary, then the one-day-a-century exercise would be superfluous, because Death could have gotten the same info by asking any recently deceased person the same questions.

In this conversation, we can see it being reiterated how important it is to seize the moments when you can. And in Didi's response we can see evidence of the ambivalence people may often feel towards life (as it is always a race against time) and Didi's feeling that she didn't get to experience enough of it.

Death's one-day-a-century is the only time she gets to enjoy the little moments of mortal existence that we experience through our sensory organs. That means she only has one day to enjoy as many little moments as she can. Given the near infinite variety of little moments that one could experience (especially if we include all non-human existences), Death is also racing against time. She's trying to squeeze as many as she can into each day, and it probably feels as if there will never be enough days to experience it all.

One efficient way of keeping this feeling fresh in Death's consciousness is to put her in the thick of things on a regular basis.

It may even be the *only* way to drive this lesson home, but that depends on whether or not you think it's impossible to know someone else's subjective experience.

9
Coming of Age with the Ageless

WADE NEWHOUSE

When I first read *The Graveyard Book*, I thought of it as a typical coming-of-age story with some ghosts thrown in for spooky effect. We've all grown up with stories like this: a precocious child grows up among his family members (foster families are even better) and must learn about both his own unique identity and the rules and expectations of the larger society in which he finds himself. Because that larger society happens, in the case of Gaiman's novel, to be populated by dead people, Bod's identity and those rules and expectations are somewhat unearthly, but the story's structure is familiar and the ending is appropriately satisfying: Bod leaves behind the community he has known and prepares to enter a larger and more complex world as a young adult.

Another way to read *The Graveyard Book* is to think of it as a traditional Gothic ghost story with coming-of-age elements thrown in for structure and moral effect. We've probably all seen stories like this, too—or at least the movies based on them: a relatively everyday-type person comes into contact with a supernatural presence, usually while confined to a somewhat restrictive spooky location that seems separated from normal time. As the character learns more about this haunted setting, they also learn some important (not always pleasant) things about their own identity. In this case, Bod needs the denizens of the graveyard to teach him not only basic survival skills but the secrets of his destiny and the basic facts of human mortality. By the end, we see that ghosts are necessary to Bod's psychological growth because they represent uncomfortable truths not easily confronted in the land of the living.

But what if we don't privilege either the coming-of-age story OR the ghost story and we read *The Graveyard Story* through the lenses of both popular genres at the same time? There are plenty of interesting similarities in the two types of stories, especially as they help us understand some essential ideas about what it means to have a "self."

For both traditional coming-of-age stories and literary ghost stories, the whole purpose of the plot is to let the protagonist come to grips with new (or previously hidden) dimensions of their character. For both types of stories, the resolution of the story depends on the protagonist's eventual acceptance of themselves in all their messy and often inconclusive glory. Finally—and most important for *The Graveyard Book*—stories of growing up and stories of hauntings focus on how the protagonist confronts a system of rules and social norms. The "self" that both genres hopes to reveal at the end is visible, in fact, almost entirely through the main character's troubled relationship with what *other* people expect of them and how they react to those constraints.

Some of the best-known novels in the Gothic ghost tradition prominently feature children—or perhaps adults who think like children—alongside their ghosts. Steven Bruhm has pointed out that "contemporary Gothic characters often utterly confuse their childhood experiences with their adult lives." Children, in this tradition, represent a somewhat uncomfortable place where the memory of innocence and the temptations of adult depravity come together. Being haunted in these books is really less about the scares provided by the ghosts and more about the scares provided by the adult psyche when it transgresses important social and moral lines that typically aren't spoken of and shouldn't be crossed.

The Graveyard Book is fully aware of this tradition and calls upon it at important moments in Bod's journey. However, because *The Graveyard Book* is *also* a coming-of-age story, it has a competing interest in "important social and moral lines" as borders that *must* be discussed and confronted for an adult self to develop. Much of the fun of Gaiman's novel, then, comes from the way it playfully challenges the "lessons" that come from both ghost stories and growing-up stories. What we get at the end in Bod's farewell to the graveyard is a new philosophy of the self that is far less interested in polite acceptance of social stability and conformity than either of its parent genres would be comfortable with.

Kids and Knowledge

From Frances Hodgson Burnett's *The Secret Garden* to E.B. White's *Charlotte's Web* to Katherine Paterson's *Bridge to Terabithia* to the recent epics of Harry Potter and Percy Jackson, the essential heart of coming-of-age stories is a young person learning first about their own unique identity and then about how to be that self in a world whose rules and expectations seem insurmountable. While such stories are set in every time and place in history and off into an imaginary future, most tales of pre-teen intellectual and moral growth tend to use the external conditions of a particular social system to chart the internal evolutions of the young person.

All these stories (and countless others) depend on two key points that Gaiman's novel treats with playful respect. The first is that children don't properly have a real "self" until they create one out of their interactions with the outside world. The second is that this process of self-creation can only occur by learning and ultimately respecting a system of rules and limitations. Even the most free-spirited kids must eventually learn "their place" in a world that is much bigger than they are.

The characters who become the happiest and best-adjusted have learned by the end of their stories what they can and cannot do, even if (as in we might remember from our own pre-teen perspectives) those restrictions are unjust and immoral. Bod's growth follows the typical pattern but is complicated (and made that much more fun to read) by the fact that he has two different societies to come to grips with.

Most of *The Graveyard Book* is about what Bod learns from his dead and undead friends, and the relationship between their standards of appropriate behavior in day-to-day "life" and the rules of the outside world is not always clear or direct. If stories about young people have a social value partly because their fictional characters model appropriate behavior for their readers' own developing social awareness, then it's hard to know exactly what kinds of lesson we should take from Bod's adventures. Is a quietly vampiric loner like Silas really the best mentor for a kid who wants to know how to make good decisions at school or in the neighborhood? *The Graveyard Book* ends before we have seen Bod really applying the lessons of the dead to the living world, and it's not at all clear to me just what he is prepared for in a life without access to ghoul-gates and fading. To a large extent, the book's climax asks us to judge his social fitness for ourselves.

When we follow a story, we draw upon certain assumptions about what a story can be. A popular Hollywood movie, for instance, whether it was made in the 1940s or the 1990s, can be expected to have a hero, a conflict, probably some romantic entanglements, and some kind of unambiguous "happy" or "sad" ending. There are literally endless possibilities for movie plotlines, but we expect some basic adherence to this formula (and some audiences cannot imagine a story on the screen to be told any other way)—and that is because we have developed a sort of *metanarrative* about the kinds of stories movies should tell.

This metanarrative is what lets us recognize the basic values of Bod's story—his desire to fit into society, his process of learning to use his powers, his quest for an understanding of himself. To some degree, all stories of young people in our culture follow this formula; only the scenery is different from story to story.

Jean-François Lyotard claims, however, that our postmodern society no longer accepts such metanarratives at face value. As technology and information exchange become more important to social progress than old paradigms of manufacturing goods and learning facts, the complex web of relationships between knowledge, teachers, and learners begins to break down. Individuals begin to see themselves as less dependent on "big picture" stories and more responsible for creating their own ideas out of the fragments produced by an endlessly expanding network of other people's individual ideas. Perhaps the best illustration of such postmodern identity-building is the internet.

For thinkers most comfortable with the notion that some kind of permanent bond—of family, nation, or religious tradition—gives us meaning, this new situation can seem threatening. As Lyotard summarizes the potential crisis of faith: "Each individual is referred to himself. And each of us knows that our *self* does not amount to much" (p.15).

This is perhaps the way all young people in coming-of-age stories must feel, and I think Bod must feel it even more keenly, since for most of the novel he is literally the only one of his kind within his visible world. His self really does not amount to much, especially in the presence of ghouls and were-wolves and (later) murderous Jacks. As we shall see, Lyotard eventually argues that this postmodern condition contains the seeds of powerful individualization rather than nihilistic despair, and Bod will show us how that happens.

Dancing through Death

First, though, we need to keep in mind another lesson that children teach us in their coming-of-age stories: sooner or later, we must all accept the reality of death.

If stories about growing up are largely about accepting and working within systems of rules, death may be the ultimate unbreakable rule—the one limitation that links all societies and communities and historical settings.

When I was a kid, we all cried when Bambi's mother died, and we couldn't believe that Charlotte the spider would die before her precious eggs hatched. To this day, you will not get me to watch movies like *Old Yeller* or *Where the Red Fern Grows* (stories about dog deaths tend to really get to me). To borrow Lyotard's vocabulary, you might say that accepting death is one of the most basic metanarratives that we have as human beings. However, this is where Bod's development in *The Graveyard Book* starts to depart a bit from the traditional pattern—because while a deep understanding and acceptance of death's inevitability is most often the final lesson a child must learn, for Bod it is the first lesson.

For Bod, it's life—not death—that is the mystery. Bod lives daily on the impossible side of the greatest taboo that most people will ever confront. Because of this simple fact, the larger philosophical confrontation with death as a source of self-knowledge is already to some degree unavailable to Bod, and that makes the "moral" of *The Graveyard Book* less clear than it typically is in coming-of-age novels. Part of the system by which we have traditionally given meaning to our lives comes from a belief in teleology—the belief that our life story is going somewhere in a particular, understandable direction. As the undisputed end of that story, death provides the necessity to find meaning and structure in the life that precedes it. Like everything else when seen through a postmodern lens, however, even death must be seen not as an absolute entity but as a relationship between ideas.

Like other traditional characters, Bod lives out his story by learning lessons about what he can and cannot do, and (more importantly) what he should and should not do. From the beginning, typically, he complains about these constraints. His first spoken life of dialogue in the novel is "Why amn't I allowed out of the graveyard?" (p. 35), and he follows this up with the pouty insistence that he wants to be like his apparently-undead guardian Silas, who has the enviable freedom to come and go as he pleases. Later, he complains about having to eat his teacher Miss Lupescu's food, grumbles through his Fading lessons, and goes against his elders' suggestion to avoid the unconsecrated ground where the witch lies buried. Though he doesn't realize the meaning of the act at the time, he takes his place among the living rather than the dead when he participates in the Danse Macabre.

In this eerie scene, Bod discovers that on the rare occasions when winter flowers bloom in the graveyard, the ghosts are free to leave their haunts and join the local townspeople in a public dance—one that the living do not remember afterward but are driven by tradition to repeat. This episode, which appears about halfway through the novel, explains how fully both the living and the dead must adhere to certain universal rules and governing structures. "Everything in its season," notes Silas when Bod chooses this day to push more questions about what the future might bring (p. 150). Though the dead look forward to their rare opportunity to mingle with the living, the living townspeople approach the ritual with a sense of automated foreboding; the Lady Mayoress suggests "vaguely" that her distributing of the fragile flowers is "Some sort of tradition," one which they all must follow without knowing why (p. 154). Bod, who has had little personal contact with anyone in his short life, is enchanted by the ensuing spectacle, "a line dance that had been ancient a thousand years before" (p. 159).

The dance, then, is more than simply one more strange episode in Bod's endlessly strange life. It represents both an inescapable, primal need (both living and dead are powerless to avoid it) and a ritualized demarcation of differences, borders, and absolutes. Silas, neither alive nor dead, is not permitted to dance; Bod, though he stays for much of the novel unsure of his place in the world, finds himself eagerly joining the living side of the spectacle (where of course he ultimately belongs).

The significance of Bod's participation becomes clear at the end of the scene, when the ghost of Josiah Worthington refuses to acknowledge that the event ever occurred:

> The dead and the living do not mingle, boy. We are no longer part of their world; they are no part of ours. If it happened that we danced the danse macabre with them, the dance of death, then we would not speak of it, and we certainly would not speak of it to the living.

When Bod protests that he is still "one of you," Josiah Worthington sniffs, "Not yet, boy. Not for a lifetime." After hearing this, "Bod realized why he had danced as one of the living, and not as one of the crew that had walked down the hill" (p. 163).

It might be tempting to say that this scene celebrates absolutes—that it finds comfort in the obvious separation between living and dead that represents all kinds of other absolutes. But that reading would be to miss the point of Bod's own flexibility, which is where the emotion of the scene lies. Commenting again on the nature of the self as the place where knowledge is created and passed on, Lyotard notes that "no self is an island; each exists in a fabric of relations that is now more complex and mobile than ever before. Young or old, man or woman, rich or poor, a person is always located at 'nodal points' of specific communication circuits" (p.15).

This description of society as a network of connections rather than unique, spiritual identities emphasizes both the universality of our participation in society (as the Danse Macabre also does) and the fact that we need others to see our own place. Or, to put it another way, our own place is always shifting as those around us move to their own rhythm. Bod's power—both in the story and as a story to be told—is his ability to experiment with such moments of contact rather than to seek out a single place and stay there.

Ghosts and What They Reveal

Scenes such as the Danse Macabre remind us that despite Bod's resemblance to typical children in traditional stories about growing up, Bod's sense of self develops within a framework dictated by ghosts and a supernatural attitude toward rules and borders. There are rules in *The Graveyard Book*, but Bod has a unique ability to push those rules to their limits— after all, he can observe the dance from the sidelines before participating, can speak directly to the Grim Reaper-esque Lady on the Grey, and is willing to talk about the whole thing afterwards.

To better understand how the presence of ghosts affects Bod's growth from one rule-driven society in the graveyard to another in the real world, we need to really look at what ghosts DO in their own stories. In literary and psychological terms, ghosts signify some things about selfhood and moral development that significantly enrich our understanding of Bod's growth. In novels, unlike folk tales and urban legends, ghosts tend to be personal; they do not haunt indiscriminately, but appear to specific individuals who come to the story already burdened by some kind of inner turmoil that comes from a confrontation with social expectations.

At the risk of being unnecessarily creepy, if you *have* any real-life ghost story experiences, compare them to the literary ghosts I discuss in this chapter. The question is whether the haunting is about the haunted *place* (which is typically the case in the more famous "real" ghost stories) or about *you* (which is what the fiction is really interested in).

Bod's ghosts don't work quite this way (they are not literally haunting anyone), but they serve some of the same purpose as their more Gothic ancestors. For now, we'll briefly consider a great ghost story from a very different era that might be said to have established the rules for literary ghosts: Henry James's *The Turn of the Screw* (1898). This is a story about "haunted" adults, but it insists that part of *being* a haunted adult is wrapped up in the kind of moral language that seems more appropriate when talking about children. Examining what childishness and ghosts have to do with one another will help us see how Gaiman's novel twists this tradition for its own ends.

Stephen King's *Danse Macabre* is a great resource for understanding the philosophy behind literary ghosts. In this very readable analysis of horror pop culture between the 1950s and 1980s, horror icon Stephen King explains how ghosts (especially in haunted houses) feed on narcissism, "a growing obsession with one's own problems" (p. 281)[1]. While King primarily uses this concept to explore more recent novels such as Shirley Jackson's *The Haunting of Hill House* and Peter Straub's *Ghost Story*, he alludes to those novels' indebtedness to *The Turn of the Screw* before them, as well as James's influence on King's own novel *The Shining* a generation later.

What all of these novels have in common is not simply the haunted house or the ghosts that might reside there but the psychology of the character who experiences those ghosts. In each case, the hauntings begin when the protagonist finds him- or herself pushed to the edge of their ability to deal with rules that govern social or moral standards of behavior.

The Turn of the Screw tells the story of a strait-laced Victorian governess who believes that the ghosts of her predecessor and that woman's secret lover are trying to corrupt the two children in her charge. The beauty of the book is that we are never sure that there are any ghosts at all—we hear about the experience in the governess's own elliptical voice, and her descriptions of the spirits often sound more like a person undergoing therapy than someone experiencing a good haunting. "I felt I was ready for more," says the governess when she believes she sees a ghost watching her; "Then I again shifted my eyes—I faced what I had to face."

The ghosts (if there are any) are less a real presence than the psychic manifestations of the governess's own struggles with class status and sexuality. She becomes convinced that she must "protect" the children from some quality of these ghosts that she herself is unable to articulate, because the ghosts testify to the reality of desires and frustrations that good Victorian society isn't allowed to talk about. "They know—

---

[1] King's terminology is based on his paraphrasing of an article by John G. Park published in *Critique* in 1978.

it's too monstrous!" she cries when she perceives that the children might have seen the ghosts as well; "they know, they know!" (p. 328).

This novel—really the story on which all modern ghost stories are based—clearly links the presence of ghosts to knowledge, specifically knowledge of firm social boundaries and the unspeakable possibilities of what might lie beyond them. The governess pursues "the strange steps of my obsession" to keep the children from knowing about things that we suspect *she* is not emotionally equipped to handle (p. 356). The lady might be said to protest too much.

Ghosts as Educators

There's a lot more going on in books about ghosts, of course, and scholars have read all kinds of different "meanings" in these hauntings. What clearly drives such stories, however, is a particular relationship between ghosts and people—and perhaps more broadly between the living and the dead—in which ghosts call attention to the "unfinished" parts of a character's personality.

Even though a book like *The Turn of the Screw* is not a "children's book," the ghosts in that story function very much as fairy tales do for children, expressing, as Alison Lurie says, "whatever is muted, suppressed, or compromised in mainstream culture." Specifically, the ghosts alert us to the ways in which such characters fail to measure up to social and cultural norms. Long before she meets any evidence of ghosts, James's heroine is already haunted by sexuality and by her own economic condition; she is afraid of her own emotions and her own social place. Once she believes that there are ghosts to confront, the governess finds she has something to talk about and something to say; more importantly, she has a mission, something to do for the first time. "I now saw that I had been asked for a service admirable and difficult," she explains (p. 325).

The Graveyard Book expands and heightens this element of ghostly fiction by letting Gaiman's own immature protagonist confront not one but many ghosts, each of them representing a tiny slice of history, a particular way of looking at the world that has led us to the present day. From the Roman Caius Pompeius to the witch Liza Hempstock, and from spinster

Letitia Borrows to Thackeray Porringer, Bod's ghosts embody not the psychological nerves of a particular moment in history but the interrelated network of lessons and learning that is human history itself. It's easy to feel, as Bod sometimes does, that time and history are too large to get a handle on, and that we are insignificant in the larger scheme of things.

In a place where dead Romans and eighteenth-century poets can give equally valid advice simultaneously—and can thrust themselves into the cat-and-mouse game upon which Bod's life depends—history and its lessons must be considered anew. The excitement and unpredictability of *The Graveyard Book*'s climactic chase comes from the way Bod asserts his own strength and cunning by working with—rather than escaping from—the continuing influence of the past that is represented by the ghosts. To fight evil, that episode teaches us, is to pick and choose lessons from a wide range of historical personalities and moralities. The graveyard does not present a unified philosophical or cultural "truth"; it does not tell a particular meta-narrative. If traditional ghosts serve a cultural purpose by marking out a specific location of social tension, a scary emotional place where the intention to follow rules slides into the temptation to over-energetically assert a powerful selfhood, the sheer number of ghosts in Gaiman's novel suggests that those social boundaries are almost too numerous to keep track of.

Where classic ghost stories seem relentless in their depiction of the process by which haunted individuals move toward a confrontation with self-knowledge, *The Graveyard Book* shows such knowledge emerging almost randomly, time and again, in different historical dialects and exhibiting a wide range of potentially conflicting values (Nehemieh Trot, after all, just hopes to get a great ode out of Bod's battle with Jack!).

Your Self: On the Line

Stories about children becoming adults expect their heroes to grow into society's standards, while ghost stories are looking for ways to punish those who cannot recognize the lines or who cross them haphazardly to serve their own weak or selfish ends. Coming-of-age stories set their characters up to prove their strength and resilience; ghost stories set *their* protagonists up to fail.

The Graveyard Book comes up with something original by combining these patterns, and the end result suggests an entirely different way of looking at how social rules and community standards work in the first place. For one thing, there are really two different communities in Gaiman's novel—the graveyard itself and the outside "real" world that Bod only occasionally interacts with. As the Danse Macabre episode insists, the worlds of the living and the dead are NOT mirror images of one another and they do not easily work together. In other words, I think the most important thing to realize about Bod's coming-of-age story is that by the end of the book he *hasn't* yet proven his ability to survive among us. His brief foray into public school is a nightmare, he has almost literally sent the only human adults he knows straight to Hell, and his only close friend must have her memory erased so she can function again after the battle with the Jacks. What, exactly, has Bod learned?

What he has learned is a lesson that goes against the grain of both the young adult genre and the ghost story genre: that limits and rules and boundaries can and must be *violated* rather than preserved or adopted. Remember that the entire reason for the Jacks of All Trades to pursue Bod in the first place is that he fulfills the prophecy of "a child born who would walk the borderland between the living and the dead" (p. 271).

Bod's guardian Silas admits, in the book's final pages, that he himself has a responsibility to "protect the borders of things"—but he admits this only as he gives Bod some money and sends him on his way out of the graveyard. Does Silas perhaps realize that some borders cannot be protected? The qualities of Bod's character—what we regard as his real "self" by the end of the story—are the qualities that go against what he has been taught by the ghosts. He befriends an outcast witch and risks his life to get her a gift; he uses his graveyard powers to wreak vengeance against the school kids who threaten him; he takes his battle against the Jacks to them on his own terms.

As readers, we root for all these actions, yet the values we cheer for here are not those he has learned in the graveyard. Jill P. May has observed that "youthful readers feel strong alliances to protagonists who deal with complex situations and act in admirable ways," and in the case of *The Graveyard Book* this means that young readers align themselves with a character who not only survives all of his societal transgressions but *gets to leave the entire system behind at the end of the story*.

The Graveyard Book is filled with elements that might be conceivable but not, in a realistic story, presentable. The ghosts are of course the first such element. Gaiman's ghosts, because of their collective ability to offer competing worldviews and direction, point toward a process of conversation rather than a specific resolution. As Josiah Worthington remarks when Bod first comes to live among them, the dead's duty is not to any particular moral or emotional priority but "to the graveyard, and to the commonality of those who form this population" (p.22).

Typical children's literature might reward a spunky kid (think anyone from Junie B. Jones for little ones to, of course, Harry Potter for the tweens and teens) but everyone knows that the protagonist's can-do spirit will serve him or her well in the real world. But what "real world" is Bod going off to join? We never see it. Whatever Neil Gaiman's personal philosophy might be about good and evil or justice and cruelty in our world, *The Graveyard Book* doesn't say much about it.

This is not to say that there are no basic human values being asserted here. Gaiman cuts through expected good-versus-evil paradigms with pretty broad strokes. Despite their somewhat lofty metaphysical goals, the Jacks first appear in the book murdering an innocent family; the "bad guys" in Bod's school episodes are typical bullies. A simple respect for others seems to be Gaiman's guiding moral light, the basic humanity that links the fates of the living to the memories of the dead. The graveyard's treatment of Liza Hempstead, however, stands out as a grim reminder that it's tricky to impose our own contemporary sensibilities backward onto history. Silas, too, admits that he has had his own murderous past. Even our best friends have dark sides.

Yet we believe we're witnessing in the story of Bod Owens the story of a moral development; he seems like a good guy. Gaiman presents a vision of postmodern moral growth based on accepting divergent viewpoints and accepting their contradictions, limitations, and eccentricities as the very essence of selfhood. In the end, Bod's proudest statement of his own awareness of self sounds ironically like a denial of self: "I'm Nobody Owens. That's who I am" (p. 282).

By announcing that he will be "nobody," Bod symbolically claims ownership of an identity that is at once autonomous and universal—he is most himself by being generic, by being no one at all. In traditional moral societies—such as those that are so often depicted and enforced in children's literature and ghost stories—such a statement would announce a serious crisis. Imagine, for instance, if the spider web in *Charlotte's Web* had announced that Wilbur was not "some pig" but "*just* some pig"!

When Bod leaves the graveyard behind, it remains as it always was—Bod's transgressions have protected and developed *him*, but they have not affected the timeless progression of historical movement that his friends from Caius Pompeius to Nehemiah Trot represent. Furthermore, Bod understands deeply what many normal people still can't wrap their heads around: the fact that he too will someday "return to the graveyard or ride with the Lady on the broad back of her great grey stallion" (p. 307).

So, the most basic rules and boundaries are both evadable and permanent. Slipping past the moral assessments of both children's literature and Gothic horror, *The Graveyard Book* ultimately suggests that actual "Life"—which is what the final line claims Bod will finally encounter—is an entirely personal experience to be found not in the acceptance of others' standards of conduct but the inevitably creative, unknowable movement beyond them.[2]

---

[2] I'd like to thank my 2010 Children's Literature class at William Peace University for all their insights into *The Graveyard Book* and its relationship to so many other stories. My students helped me put these ideas in order and offered great suggestions that are too numerous to include in this chapter.

10
Hell Can Be Good for You

NAJWA AL-TABAA

What would happen if Lucifer decided to close Hell? A lot of damage, to say the least. Well, that's exactly what happens in *The Sandman: Season of Mists*. Lucifer's abandonment of Hell leaves its governance up for grabs, and every demon wants a piece.

Season of Mists ends with the Angels taking control of Hell. They want to transform Hell into a place of "good," a place where punishment leads to redemption. Why change Hell at all? It seems pretty hellish as it is, with its fire and brimstone, eternal suffering, and, I feel sure, a constant soundtrack of Justin Bieber. It all begins when Morpheus is reminded by The Endless of his unspeakable act in condemning his once beloved Nada to Hell. Death reminds Morpheus of the "terrible" and "appalling" thing he did to poor Nada. This guilt spurs Morpheus's quest and return to Hell.

Ready for a hell of a fight, Morpheus confronts Lucifer, only to find that he's in no mood to fight. Hell is being undone and reshaped. Handing over the keys, Lucifer burdens Morpheus with the worst punishment of all, being in charge of Hell. Hell morphs into a place of redemption intended to mirror Heaven rather than the place of insurmountable punishment. The shift from punishment to redemption not only destabilizes Hell but is grounded in forgiveness, which seems like a solution but only generates more problems for the prisoners of Hell.

Jacques Derrida states in *On Cosmopolitanism and Forgiveness* that, "forgiveness forgives only the unforgivable. One cannot or should not forgive; there is only forgiveness, if there is any, where there is the unforgivable." What he is saying is that the only possible thing that is truly forgivable is something that is so atrociously awful that forgiving it seems unimaginable, like being condemned to Hell by a former lover.

Morpheus's realization of his horrible behavior towards Nada leads to the eventual unraveling of Hell. The inhabitants of Hell are unable to get forgiveness for themselves and for the acts they committed. They have all committed unforgivable sins, after all. They want to be punished because they feel they deserve punishment, not forgiveness. Lucifer reveals to the Dream Lord that the inhabitants of Hell only receive the punishment that they themselves desire and request. As Lucifer releases the inmates of Hell, he gives them a semblance of forgiveness, but not true forgiveness, partly because he isn't the one who could *ever* forgive them. Lucifer had never been wronged by them.

True forgiveness, according to Derrida is forgiving that which is unforgiveable. He creates a paradox with this statement. This idea creates the concept that forgiveness can only happen to and for acts that are considered unforgiveable. People forgive each other all the time for trivial things. For Derrida, this makes the act of forgiving less valuable. If forgiveness is the same for stealing a few dollars and killing someone, or even for mass genocide, then the act of forgiveness loses its value.

We dismiss the admiration of people who gape at and compliment everything that someone does, because the compliments don't feel genuine, when they are given for everything. Forgiveness can suffer from the same fate when it is offered so easily. Like an over-issued currency, overuse of forgiveness depreciates forgiveness. Derrida creates a paradox by claiming that the only real form of forgiveness is forgiving that which is unforgiveable, in order to preserve the value of forgiving. So the value in forgiveness is dependent on the person doing the forgiving rather than the one receiving the forgiveness. In *Season of Mists*, the Angels Duma and Remiel, who become the interim guardians of Hell, rebuild it so that the damned aren't punished, but instead given the opportunity for redemption; a shot at being forgiven for their unforgivable sins.

Forgiving over Punishment

After Lucifer closes Hell, the inhabitants stay! The damned feel the need to continue to be punished for their crimes on Earth. Forgiveness is only possible when both parties, the unforgiven and the forgiver, allow it. Morpheus wants to be forgiven, and Nada is willing to forgive him after she is released from her undeserved punishment. In this case, punishment has helped bring about the conditions which makes forgiveness possible. If what Nada was forgiving Morpheus for was something minor, spilling water on her kitchen floor, then there would be no real need for punishment. Forgiveness could be given immediately but this sort of "wrong" is precisely the kind of wrong that Derrida says we should not be forgiving. Such acts could simply be ignored or overlooked. Only the unforgivable can be forgiven because the essence of forgiveness can only be understood through the unforgivable.

Perhaps unforgivable acts require some kind of punishment before they can be forgiven. Morpheus's 'punishment' is the awareness that he has wronged Nada. I use 'punishment' here in quotes, because it isn't quite the same as the punishment that is normally thought of as being dealt out in Hell. Let's call it "the cost of redemption" for the lack of a better word. Morpheus, one of the Endless, *the Lord of Dream*, screwed up. In releasing Nada, Morpheus admits his error. Nada, showing *endless* compassion, is really the enlightened being, by recognizing the difficulty of what Morpheus is doing, and allows him to be forgiven.

The alternative would be to punish Morpheus endlessly. Refuse to forgive him. Sending Nada to Hell for refusing to be his lover shows his arrogance and callousness. Why not burden him with some guilt, seeing that Nada was burdened with damnation? As Lucifer and Morpheus walk the vast lands of Hell, they encounter a lingering soul. Lucifer tells this soul he's got to go, Hell is closed, not "back in five minutes closed," but totally closed. The soul tells Lucifer, "You . . . Do . . . Not Understand. I am Breschau." And Lucifer responds with "So?"

The response is twisted because it illustrates the meaninglessness of punishment. The punishment, the crimes, the prisoners are all meaningless. Lucifer wants to quit being the caretaker of Hell, in part because he recognizes the pointlessness of the task. Unforgivable sins, require eternal punishment. Forgiveness on the other hand, having the chance to be redeemed from the sins one has committed, has a clear goal; an end. While punishment is insurmountable, forgiveness offers hope and possibly redemption.

Punishment can't be a necessary condition for forgiveness, since it is without meaning. Punishment can be a catalyst since it plays on our ability to empathize, while also ensuring that a degree of justice has been accomplished. However, this degree varies from victim to victim. Who's to say when punishment is enough, or that forgiveness is possible? The victims must decide. But in Hell, do the Angels speak for the victims? If not, for whom do they speak?

The new Hell is created out of the idea of forgiveness and the Angels want to it to be a place of redemption. Once the prisoners forgive themselves, the redemptive and healing process happens, or so the Angels hope. But the prisoners resist this change. In our real world, the prison system pursues rehabilitation: prisons are not merely for punishing lawbreakers, but also to give them the opportunity to be redeemed for their past wrongs. Is Hell trying to reach that same ideal? Is it even possible in the real world? The sinner's resistance to rehabilitation suggests that it may not be possible to maintain that ideal. It needs to be a collaborative effort between those imprisoned and those dealing out the punishment. The sinners in Hell have to want to be redeemed for this philosophy of forgiveness to work.

The Cost of Redemption

In Michel Foucault's book *Discipline and Punish: The Birth of the Prison* he points to the history of punishment as being a spectacle. Pain and suffering were supposed to be visually displayed on the prisoner's body. The reformatory, where the goal is reformative punishment, is not yet imagined in the pre-nineteenth century that Foucault speaks of. The new reformative prison system focuses creating a redemptive change in the prisoners' "souls."

A prisoner's perception of himself or herself is shaped by the redemptive aspect of the prison system. The Panopticon was an ideal prison imagined by Jeremy Bentham. The design of the Panopticon creates the feeling that everyone is being constantly watched. Bentham hoped a sense of self-government and self-control would develop because of the psychological element of being constantly watched. Ultimately, this would make a prisoner into a better person by strengthening their ability to control their more base impulses. This system puts the responsibility for rehabilitation onto the individual prisoner rather than on the outside sources of punishment in the form of pain and torture.

The Angels at the end of *Season of Mists* seek to change Hell by having the inhabitants engage in redemption rather than punishment, but is their brand of redemption really all that different from punishment? The inhabitants of Hell feel they deserve their punishment. Gaiman writes that "indeed, had Hell been pleasant, they would have felt cheated: They were there for pain, for suffering, for torment, which they received in abundance" (p. 39).

The Angels re-evaluate the function of punishment by creating a new goal for it. In Foucault's argument, the re-evaluated goal of a prison is to create an environment that also allows prisoners to regain, or maintain, a sense of humanity on an individual level. This leads to the obvious question: why should we care about their humanity? They've done unforgivable acts!

Aurora Levins-Morales, a Latin American feminist writer and advocate of social justice, writes about the concept of forgiveness and the capacity for forgiving "ourselves" and "our perpetrators." She claims that, "healing takes place in community, in the telling and the bearing witness, in the naming of trauma and in the grief and rage and defiance that follow." This sense of communal healing is what the Angels want to institute in Hell, which requires an affirmation of the value, the basic humanity, of the damned. Levin-Morales writes that in enduring inhumane conditions "it's a struggle for the imaginations of the oppressed people, for our capacity to see ourselves as human when we are being treated inhumanly."

But do these Angels really have the best interest of the prisoners in mind? The Angels certainly believe that they are serving some higher purpose and helping the prisoners by instituting the new system, regardless of whether it is welcome.

The Angels' new world order is thrust upon the prisoners just as much as their punishment was before. In this remodeled Hell, there is an absence of communication between the Angels and the prisoners. The prisoners' voices and wants are not heard, which consequently devalues their humanity. Yes, being in prison, or Hell, does limit certain individual rights, but if the goal is to create a more redemptive space, neglecting to consider the perspective of the prisoners is changing things only superficially, and ironically limits the possibility of redemption. Derrida says that "when the victim and guilty share no language, when nothing common and universal permits them to understand one another, forgiveness seems deprived of meaning." The Angels want redemption in Hell, but what does everyone else want? Ignoring the prisoner's desires, ignores their humanity, which is the exact thing that redemption aims to rescue.

Before Redemption Comes Compassion

In the end of *Season of Mists* the Angels strive to reinvent Hell. They want to "help" the inmates of Hell achieve redemption. The Angels announce: "No, . . . That was the old Hell. That was a place of mindless torture and purposeless pain. There will be no more wanton violence; no further suffering, inflicted without reason or explanation . . . we will hurt you. And we are not sorry. But we do not do it to punish you. We do it to redeem you. Because afterward, you'll be a better person . . . and because we love you. One day, you'll thank us for it" (p. 216).

The Angels do not show the inmates of Hell compassion because they don't understand their desire for endless punishment; the proposed system of redemption becomes altruistic. The inmates of Hell will supposedly thank the Angels for the sense of salvation and redemption created through the redesign of Hell as a space of redemption. The doomed souls and inmates of Hell react to the Angels by saying "But...You don't understand...that makes it worse. That makes it so much worse. . . ." (p. 217). In trying to reinvent Hell, the Angels simply recreate Hell, with a façade of doing good.

If compassion is necessary for forgiveness, then pain and suffering is necessary because they are the objects of compassion. There is a hierarchy of pain; some pain is just more compelling than other pain. Not any pain will do for redemption.

It's now clearer why the damned prefer Lucifer's Hell to the Angels' Hell. Which is worse—an eternity spent striving for redemption or an eternity accepting despair? Punishment's easier to accept, redemption is much more complicated. Punishment is passive; the prisoners receive punishment, but redemption requires interaction and a desire to rebuild. The souls of Hell seem to be more willing to accept punishment and an eternity of despair than suffering through the struggle for redemption.

We need to think of justice and judgment in the visceral sense, which is where the concept of compassion comes in. The visceral sense of compassion and redemption is what the inmates of Hell want to avoid—they'd rather just take the insurmountable torture and pain than be faced with a reflective understanding of the wrongs they have done. Hell is not just a fictional place; we have Hell on Earth, the prison system. The points that Gaiman makes at the end of *Season of Mists* demonstrate how even when it seems as if the goals of running Hell, or the prison system, seem to be redemption, in reality it more complicated. Just like the Angels, "we"—society—are doing our best to be Angels running Hell. Much like Hell and the Angels, our prison systems seek to rehabilitate through punishment, or so it seems.

The inmates of Hell seem to feel that despair is the better option and are unwilling to commit to a punishment that yields the possibility of redemption, and so consequently only get punishment, and since this isn't Hell, it isn't eternal punishment. Even if the Angels are just trying to do their best to help the inmates, and even if their methods and reasoning might be altruistic, the obstacle they must face is a group of people who would rather endure an eternity of despair than work towards redemption.

At the end of *Season of Mists*, Hell has begun to change, or so the Angels believe. Redemption has been substituted for damnation, and correction has been substituted for despair. The flames of Hell have now become "refining" flames creating "purity" and "good" (p. 217). But is this method compassion or is it just sugarcoated despair? The Angels feel that this is the way to happily ever after—a "happily ever after in Hell."

Can there be happily ever after in Hell? Hell and happiness in the same sentence just doesn't seem like a fathomable correlation, yet the Angels create for themselves a sense of happily ever after and assume that their tactics will create a happily ever after for the inmates of Hell as well. The change and destiny of Hell seems to serve the altruistic ends of the Angels. Without compassion and forgiveness happily ever after does not seem to be a likely outcome. Nada's happily ever after is not exactly ideal, but she gets a second chance at life. Perhaps this is what the hope of redemption entails—a second chance at happily ever after.

Destiny shuts the book, the story ends. What is happiness and what is happily ever after? Perhaps it is a "bloody marvelous" sunset as Lucifer admits, created by God.

11
The Dead Teach Us How to Live

WAYNE YUEN

Part of the reason why Nobody Owens is such a fascinating character is that he lives amongst the dead. Through the dead, Bod learns to live, not only a good life, but an extraordinary one with supernatural powers.

Most of us, unfortunately, have not been educated by ghosts so we don't have access to the powers that Bod has. But even without the powers of the graveyard, we can gleam quite a bit from Bod's life and apply it to our own quest for a good life.

We want to live a good life, and that means two things. First, a good life is a moral life. When we ask ourselves if we're living a good life, few people, if any, would answer "yes" if we're living an immoral one. A moral life enables us to live a good life. But just because we are living a moral life, it doesn't mean that we're living a good life, so being moral is not the only thing we need for a good life.

We don't have to look far for examples of people who have lived morally good lives, yet not lived a good life. Good people are sometimes punished for their acts, sometimes a stroke of bad luck or unfortunate circumstances will prevent good people from living good lives. So, a good life is a life that's pleasant, fulfilling, and happy. In Bod's case a stroke of bad luck came early in his life, when The man Jack came and murdered his entire family.

But wait a minute. Bod's stroke of bad luck leads him to live a good, admittedly strange and sometimes dangerous, life in the graveyard. Was it really a terrible event? I think this is the first lesson that Bod can teach us—how we're to judge the events in our life.

Bod's extraordinary life is the result of a terribly tragedy, the murder of his family by The man Jack. If this tragedy had never occurred, Bod would have grown up with his parents, and lived a perfectly ordinary life, without ever acquiring the powers of the graveyard like dreamwalking, fading, and an astonishing grasp of history. If we simply compare the life that Bod lives because of the book's opening tragedy to a relatively normal life, it's hard to argue that Bod's life is not measurably better for the unfortunate experience.

So should we say that it was a good thing for Bod's family to be murdered by The man Jack? That's clearly a ridiculous statement. Murder is not a good thing, morally, but strangely enough it leads to a qualitatively better life for Bod. This is not something unique to Bod; many people have lived lives with formative tragedies in them. When I teach ethics, I use the Nazi Holocaust as an example of a clearly bad thing; however, I've had students who tell me that if it were not for the Holocaust, they would not exist, either because their parents or grandparents met in a concentration camp, or because of other related circumstances. Many authors and Nobel laureates owe their awards, financial windfalls, and generally comfortable lives that they live today to the events of World War II. Should we say to all of these people that it's better that they live lives of quiet anonymity, or prefer non-existence, when it comes to my students, or should we say that they should be thankful for the Holocaust?

Saul Smilansky makes a helpful distinction here on the notion of being "sorry for" and "sorry that." (I owe much of what I'm saying here to Smilansky's book, *Ten Moral Paradoxes*.) Bod can be *sorry for* his parents being murdered, but is he is not obligated to be *sorry that* his parents were murdered. In this way, we can recognize both the moral tragedy of the situation and the qualitatively good or beneficial effects that the moral tragedy has had. The individuals who benefit greatly from the Holocaust, or who exist because of the Holocaust, can express moral outrage at the event, but not be committed to wanting it to have never happened, because that may mean that they wish they didn't exist.

Bod lives a life that is framed by tragedy. But these tragedies do not stop him from living a good life. Far from it, his tragic circumstances help enable him to live a good life. The fact that he has overcome such challenges and adversity, like the Holocaust survivors, isn't what makes his life a good life, it is how Bod responds to these tragedies that makes his life a good life. Lesser people may have these tragedies eclipse their lives, and who would blame them? External events have the power of ruining possibly good lives, but they are not the sole determiner of whether or not somebody has a good life. What makes Bod different? How is he able to overcome his tragedy to continue to live a good life? This leads to the second important lesson Bod has for us: a life of character.

The Dead Should Have Charity

According to the ancient Greeks, a good life was largely determined by your character. A person's character, in the view of Aristotle, is distinguished by the kinds of virtues that that person has.

Virtues are excellences of character that allow a person, or a thing, to achieve their function well. A knife's function is to cut, and sharpness would allow the knife to cut well. So, sharpness is a virtue of the knife. In order to develop our virtues, we would need to know the function, or purpose of our lives, so we would know what kinds of virtues we need in order to achieve our function well. This is where Aristotle's philosophy breaks down. He argues that there is a singular purpose for all human beings: that is, a life of intellectual inquiry. We don't need to agree with Aristotle on this point to benefit from learning what Aristotle says about virtues and applying them to our lives. Regardless of what we believe our purpose to be, or if we even deny that we have a purpose, we can all agree that there are some qualities that allow us to generally live better lives than other qualities.

Aristotle points out that virtues are not something we are born with, they are all developed through practice. Children are not particularly kind, selfless, or fair. These are virtues that they may develop over time. Bod acquires his virtues from his many teachers. His adoptive parents, Mr. and Mrs. Owens, early on teach Bod the necessity of a moral life by doing what is right, rather than what the traditions of the graveyard dictated, and caring the best they can for Bod. Mrs. Owens, in particular, thinks of caring for Bod, "doing her duty."

Bod, later, stands up to two bullies at school, Nick and Mo, not because it would be to his advantage—quite the opposite— but because it is the moral thing to do. Aristotle calls this "righteous indignation" a proper feeling of disgust and irritation in the face of injustice. Bod learns this the same way many of us learn the things that we learn, not at a formalized school, but simply living with our parents. Through repetition of example we gain their character traits, their virtues and vices. We can also try to practice particular virtues in order to acquire them on our own, or seek out those with the virtues we wish to attain, and try to be like them.

Bod has many models of virtue to choose from in the graveyard. Many ghosts are well versed in the particulars of their time, be it the virtues that were pressed at the time or historical facts. Bod knows how things really happened from firsthand accounts from those who lived through history. But factual knowledge doesn't translate into what Bod learns from Silas: wisdom, a classic Greek virtue that most people still value today. Silas is important to Bod precisely because he is wise.

> Silas brought Bod food, true, and left it in the crypt each night for him to eat, but this was as far as Bod was concerned, the least of the things that Silas did for him. He gave advice, cool, sensible, and unfailingly correct. . . .

Transforming knowledge into good advice is not something everyone can do. Plato, in particular, believes that wisdom is "good counsel," that is, being able to provide good advice or leadership.

Aristotle's list of moral virtues also include, bravery, temperance, charity, truthfulness, friendliness, wittiness, modesty, and patience. Not all of these we would consider to be *moral* virtues, like wittiness, but Aristotle believed that good characters led people to engage in good actions, and consequently people would live good lives. Wit and friendliness would allow people to make friends easily, which Aristotle believed to be an integral part of a good life, and it's not hard to see why.

When Scarlett Perkins declares Bod not a stranger, but a friend, Bod's response seems only natural. "Bod smiled rarely, but he smiled then, hugely and with delight." Friendships are intrinsically valuable, that is to say, they are valuable for their own sake, not because of the benefits we get from them, although we shouldn't dismiss what we get from them as well. Aristotle says,

> For without friends no one would choose to live, though he had all other goods; even rich men and those in possession of office and of dominating power are thought to need friends most of all; for what is the use of such prosperity without the opportunity of beneficence, which is exercised chiefly and in its most laudable form towards friends? (*Nichomachaen Ethics*, Book VIII, line 1155a5)

Liza Hempstock perhaps says it best: "Us in the graveyard, we wants you to stay alive. We wants you to surprise us and disappoint us and impress us and amaze us." Sharing our lives, and the fortunes and misfortunes we find in them, with our friends, as well as finding comfort in difficult times with them, are just some of the benefits we derive from friendship. Being entangled in other people's lives is something most people find incredibly rewarding and entertaining, despite the costs. But we don't want just anyone entangled in our lives. Our characters determine who we would like to befriend and who would befriend us. Virtuous character traits not only help us be good people, morally speaking, but also enhance the quality of our lives by enriching our lives with good friends.

Discussions of virtue often sound like conforming ourselves to a set formula of virtues. If we all adopt these virtues, wouldn't we all be the same person, cookie-cutter people without individuality? The answer is easily and emphatic, "No!" But to understand why, we need to examine one more lesson that Bod's life can give us in our search for a good life: "Authenticity."

Kiss a Lover, Dance a Measure; Find Your Name and Buried Treasure

Authenticity is *the* central virtue that the existentialists, like Sartre and Kierkegaard, argue for. Authenticity is a person being true to themselves, living life honestly, rather than pretending to be someone else by conforming to what others expect of them. Sometimes authenticity is better understood through its opposite, inauthenticity. An inauthentic life is when we conform to social norms because conforming gives us comfort, not because that is what we want to do.

Living an authentic life is difficult because many of us value the comfort that comes with conformity and if we were not to conform to social norms, we wouldn't know how to behave as "ourselves." Many people struggle at one point in their life to "find themselves" or to "discover who they are." "How can I be myself, if I don't know who I am?" is the question that arises from attempting to live an authentic life.

When Bod is first discovered by the inhabitants of the graveyard, they struggle with what to call him. Each ghost explains that Bod resembles this person or that person and should be properly called that, until Mrs. Owens interjects, "He looks like nobody but himself." Many of us can relate to the expectation of following in the footsteps of their parents' expectations, but that expectation is felt perhaps more strongly by people who are named after their parents. The suffix "Jr." or "the second" suggests a commonality between father and son, or less commonly mother and daughter.

Even people with similar names spark comparisons. When confronted with ghouls called "The 33rd President of the United States" and "The famous writer Victor Hugo," it's hard to resist the temptation of thinking about these ghouls as these figures from history. It's equally hard not to consider the future careers of the children of famous athletes and movie stars as something other than their parents. In this, Nobody Owens has a leg up on most of us, since he doesn't know his parents. He is truly a blank slate of expectation. He has nobody to become but himself.

Bod is also subjected to the call of conformity. He wants to be like Silas, his brave and wise guardian, but Silas is not like anyone else in the graveyard—he's not dead or alive. He's a vampire. When Bod says that he wants to be like his guardian, Silas tersely responds, "No, you do not." Why don't people want to be vampires? Eternal life, sexy clothes, perpetually good hair, why wouldn't Bod want to be a vampire? Silas doesn't supply an answer, but there is no need to. Bod *isn't* a vampire. Bod *is* a living boy. Silas is steering Bod away from an inauthentic life, to a life of authenticity. Bod must be himself, a living breathing human being, instead of trying to be something he is not, the living dead.

As Bod gets older, he begins to understand the distinction, even if unconsciously. In school, Mo, the bully that Bod torments through dreamwalking later, remarks that he is weird because he doesn't have any friends. Bod replies, "I didn't come here for friends. I came here to learn." Mo, understandably replies, "Do you know how weird *that* is?" Bod offers a shrug. Bod is indifferent to the call of conformity, because he's already being authentic.

A Virtuous Monster?

Referring to the The Man Jack, Bod asks, "Why didn't Silas just kill him?" Mrs. Owens replies, "He's not a monster, Bod." Silas didn't know anything about The Man Jack, nor about Bod at the time. Silas travels away from the graveyard to learn more about the threat that The Man Jack and his group of Everymen poses to Bod. Had he not, it would indeed seem rather monstrous to kill a man that he knows little or nothing about. He could have been the new night watchman or a lost tourist.

What Bod doesn't understand at this point is that the consequences of an action don't always dictate the rightness of an action. Bod is being authentic, but not wise. Indeed, had Silas killed The Man Jack earlier in the book, Bod would be safer. In fact, one would be hard pressed to imagine seriously negative consequences flowing from killing The Man Jack. Silas's action was the result of his virtues. Silas is patient and wise. Would a wise person kill a man who could be innocent? Framing questions around virtues like this can allow us to determine a course of action to take from a virtue perspective. Later when Silas and Bod fight The Man Jack and his Everymen, there's no doubt about their intentions and the danger they present. Dealing with them would be the wise action at that point in the story.

So should Bod have simply conformed his behavior to Silas's model? It really does look as if authenticity and virtue conflict with each other. However there is wiggle room to find a resolution. First, Aristotle argues that virtues are relative to the individual, that is to say, what makes one person brave, is not what would make everyone brave. It might be brave for Bod to face down The Man Jack at the climax of the story, but it would be pure foolishness for him to face The Man Jack as a toddler. It takes little bravery for Bod to stand up to Mo, but it would take a lot of bravery for Mo's terrorized classmates to stand up to her.

We can see that being virtuous does not necessarily condemn us all to be exactly the same. Include the additional virtue of authenticity and we have a wide variety of people, with motivation to be themselves. I can be authentic and brave, and not do what Silas does, because it would be foolish for me to engage in a fight with a menacing foe, but not for Silas.

Scarlett, however, sees things differently. After their encounter with the Sleer and The Man Jack, she calls Bod a monster. Bod tries to explain, but can't find the words. His actions appear monstrous to Scarlett, in part because she doesn't have the full context of the situation, and the danger that The Man Jack posed to Bod, and possibly the rest of society.

Instead of trying to explain it all, Silas wipes her memory of the events. Before he does so, Bod protests. He doesn't want Scarlett to forget him. But a better reason for not wanting her memory to be wiped is that it would be wrong. Robbing a person of their experiences, no matter how traumatic, would interfere with their authenticity. How can Scarlett be the woman who survived an encounter with the Sleer, if she doesn't know that she did? On this point Silas and Bod are at odds with each other. Bod doesn't want her memory wiped for self-interested reasons. Silas wants to wipe her memory because it would be better for her and everyone else. Scarlett demands, "Don't I get a say in this?" and it's clear that she doesn't.

Who's right here? Silas and Bod are being authentic, there is wisdom in either possibility. This is a difficult decision that has no clear right answer. I'm more sympathetic to Bod here, in that not wiping Scarlett's memory would better respect her ability to be authentic. Ideally, it would be Scarlett's choice though. Respecting her autonomy, the ability for her to choose for herself how she will live, regardless of how inconvenient that would make either Bod or Silas's life, seems to be the right call.

A Difficult Challenge, but I Can Try My Best

Living a good life isn't determined by what happens to you. It's determined by how you develop your character in response to what happens. Thinking of a good life as a life that we value for its own sake, which necessarily is a moral and authentic life. gives us a sense of empowerment. It's not fate or chance that lets some people live good lives.

We can all learn to live good lives, from those who have come before us. They don't have to be ghosts, werewolves, or vampires. We can learn to live a good life from the dead in history books, philosophy texts, and the stories of our past family members. We can learn from the living too, but the dead will always outnumber the living.

In the final analysis, we will never really know if we lived a good life, as this is something that can only be determined in retrospect, after we have lived. But our lives are our monuments to ourselves, and the better we build them, the more likely that future people will learn from our example.

Questions
of
Identity

12
Forever Batman

BRANDON KEMPNER

Neil Gaiman's brilliant take on the Dark Knight can be found in *Batman: Whatever Happened to the Caped Crusader?* Here, Gaiman attempts the impossible: he tries to write the final two issues of the Batman comic. Don't worry! It's only a literary experiment. The Batman comics continue, and will continue endlessly.

These two Gaiman issues are weird issues, crawling with bizarre takes on the Batman universe—Catwoman kills Batman! Alfred, Batman's butler, was actually the Joker!—and an unexpected conclusion that is both jarring and deeply satisfying. At the end of the volume, Batman dies and is then brought back to life as the infant Bruce Wayne, to begin the whole cycle over again. Forever Batman, eternally repeating.

Gaiman is fascinated by cycles of repetition and recurrence. He plays with recurrence and repetition throughout his works. Many of Gaiman's characters are trapped (or liberated, depending on your point of view) in cycles of repetition and recurrence. Examples include the Endless in *The Sandman*, the Eternals of *The Eternals,* the movie-maker and his thoughts of apocalypse in *Signal to Noise*, and the gods of *American Gods*.

While all of those texts are profound variations on the idea of repetition, Gaiman has made eternal recurrence the centerpiece of his *Caped Crusader*. While Batman's eternal recurrence might seem to be a punishment, Gaiman transforms this into a reward, and a profoundly life-affirming reward at that.

This repetition is what ties Neil Gaiman to Friedrich Nietzsche, who patented the idea of *eternal recurrence*. Although Nietzsche told us that God is dead, while Gaiman keeps bringing the gods back, both writers are fascinated by eternal recurrence, though it doesn't mean exactly the same in Gaiman's work as it does in Nietzsche's.

Nietzsche's idea of eternal recurrence is that the events of this life repeat themselves an endless number of times in eternally looping cycles of the same. Eternal recurrence is an idea that is both appalling—who wants an exact repetition of their life?—and strangely liberating. If life repeats endlessly, you don't have to worry about an afterlife, Heaven, Hell, transcendence, a next world. Under eternal recurrence, this life is all there is, but it never goes away.

Eternal recurrence is one of the most exciting, momentous—and unsettling—of modern philosophical concepts.[1]

What's an Overman to Do?

Nietzsche first introduced the idea of eternal recurrence with *The Gay Science*, but he fully developed the concept in his classic *Thus Spoke Zarathustra*. Previously, Nietzsche's work had concentrated on destroying old and outdated belief systems. Nietzsche's Overman (*Übermensch*) became the embodiment of someone who moved beyond conventional notions of good and evil, and who had the courage and commitment to create new values. In promoting these new value systems, Nietzsche did away with theism (belief in a deity), arguing that God and gods were man-created. "God is dead" thus became Nietzsche's rallying cry to potential Overmen, urging them to do away with the old and create the new.

If Nietzsche had turned his Overman into a comic-book character, he might very well have come up with Batman. As a masked avenger, Batman holds himself above the morality of Gotham City, and shuns conventional notions of crime-fighting. Instead, Batman invents a higher morality for himself. Separated from ordinary mankind, Batman operates as the next evolution of humanity. Such Overmen are likely to be lonely. Separated from society, and the certainty that tra-

---

[1] Ned Lukacher, *Time-Fetishes: The Secret History of Eternal Recurrence*.

ditional belief systems offer, what happens to them when they die? No God, after all, means no afterlife. Nietzsche might as well have tacked "Heaven and Hell are dead" onto his slogan.

This is where eternal recurrence comes in, as an alternative to the afterlife. As Nietzsche discarded the idea of God or gods, he also discarded the notion of a God-given end, goal, or purpose (*telos*) to life. Prior to Nietzsche, most Western philosophical systems had trumpeted a final goal to existence, whether the perfectibility of the self (Plato), the perfectibility of culture (Hegel), or the concept of Heaven (Christianity). Such systems are called *teleological* systems, since they provide meaning to human life by focusing on a final purpose or end. Teleological systems are, by their very nature, linear: a human being travels from point A (birth) to the final *telos* (Heaven, Enlightenment, perfection, transcendence).

Eternal recurrence replaces this linear, destination driven concept with a cyclical concept without a final destination. In eternal recurrence, death does not lead anywhere or to anything. Instead, you move back to the beginning of your life and repeat it down to the smallest detail: the fall of the monkey bars in the third grade, your first love, those spilled cups of coffee, those lost car keys, all the great joys and despairs of your life, all the petty annoyances.

Just think: the good, the bad, the boring, all of it exactly the same, an infinite number of times.

Frightening, isn't it?

How Bruce Learned to Love Eternal Recurrence

As crazy and off-putting as eternal recurrence might sound, Nietzsche absolutely loved the idea. Instead of a direction or purpose to life, there is only, in Nietzsche's words, "a great year of becoming, a monster of a great year, which must, like an hourglass, turn over and over again" (*Thus Spoke Zarathustra*, p. 220). This "monster of a year" is our own lives, repeated over and over. Eternal recurrence shifted attention away from the life to come, and focused attention to the life actually being lived. Teleological systems focus on destination; eternal recurrence focuses on the here and now.

Apply this idea to Batman, and you can see the crisis that Gaiman will exploit. Batman only has one ultimate outcome: he stops being Batman. Sure, that can happen a lot of ways. He can get shot. He can retire. He can get bored of being Batman. No matter what he does, though, he stops being Batman. He reaches an end. Once you've reached that end, what is Batman anymore? What did the journey mean?

Eternal recurrence gives you a way out, a way to be eternally yourself, to be always becoming. With no end—only repetition—this life continues forever.

Eternal recurrence is the perfect alternative to a teleological philosophical system. More than that, though, it was also Nietzsche's method of affirming life. In teleological systems, according to Nietzsche, humans are encouraged to look for the meaning of their lives outside of life. Since we're always looking outside of life for meaning—to the *telos* or purpose—life itself is looked down upon, as an inconvenience preventing us from reaching our final destination. According to Nietzsche, the life at hand was ignored, degraded, and rendered worthless.

For Nietzsche, the challenge of eternal recurrence was the challenge of valuing life. What kind of person would embrace eternal recurrence? For Nietzsche, this could only be someone fully satisfied with their life, someone who sees life itself, not life's final destination, as meaningful. Since most people find the idea of repeating their lives revolting, this reveals them as haters of their own lives. The truly satisfied person, according to Nietzsche, would welcome eternal recurrence. In fact, they'd demand it as the ultimate affirmation of their existence. As Nietzsche states in *Ecce Homo*, "The basic conception of the work, the *idea of eternal recurrence*," is "the highest formula of affirmation that can possibly be attained" (*Ecce Homo*, p. 69).

One of the more interesting intricacies of Nietzsche's theory is that humans never know what cycle of eternal recurrence they are caught in. This could be the first, or this could be the hundredth—or the millionth. Since you can't know, you need to live your life as positively and meaningfully as possible. If you had to repeat it an infinite number of times, would you really waste an afternoon watching bad TV? Or would you actually go out and do something with your life? This concept applies perfectly to Batman. Batman has chosen to pursue a life of fighting crime, even with everything that costs him (his family, his health) because that is the life that most satisfies him. By choosing actions that he would gladly repeat forever, Batman embraces his life.

Nietzsche's eternal recurrence is a philosophical idea that allows us to turn away from any "purpose" or "end" to life and instead affirm the act of living itself. As such, it has proven popular with a wide variety of writers, providing them with a way to celebrate the journey of their characters, not their destination. James Joyce famously used it within *Finnegans Wake*, with the novel's final sentence looping back and completing the novel's first sentence, thus turning the work into an eternally repeating ring. Gaiman himself has used the idea in several of his earlier works, such as *Signal to Noise* and *Sandman*. Gaiman's use of eternal recurrence in *Caped Crusader* is but one in a long line of eternal repetitions.

Twilight of a Superhero

The Batman story, due to the massive popularity of the comics, movies, and television shows, has become a central American myth. Like most myths, it has a beginning. In this case, that's Batman's origin story. As recounted in the early issues of *Detective Comics* or in a movie like *Batman Begins*, Bruce Wayne's parents are killed in front of him. The trauma launches him into a life of crime fighting. The Batman myth also has a middle. Batman faces off with a series of villains— Scarecrow, Joker, Two-Face, the Riddler—in his attempts to keep Gotham safe. You've also got Catwoman for romance, Alfred as a father figure, and Robin for some comic relief. Most writers of the Batman universe operate by recycling and repacking this material, telling the same stories over and over again. In this way they resemble the oral storytellers of ancient times, each putting their own spin on fundamentally the same story.

Unlike many myths, though, Batman doesn't have an end. We know how Achilles is shot in the foot and dies. Odysseus arrives back in Ithaca and lives happily ever after. What happens to Batman in the end? Does he die? Does he get thrown in jail? Go insane? Retire in comfort? Get married? Have children? Pass the Batman costume down to a successor? And which of these possible endings provides adequate meaning to Batman's life?

Providing a meaningful conclusion to the Batman story is the white whale of the comic world: a tantalizing challenge, but one that is nearly impossible. Other writers have tried: Frank Miller's *The Dark Knight Returns* gives us an aging Batman coming out of retirement one last time, and Grant Morrison's *Batman R.I.P.* and *Final Crisis* "kills" off Batman and passes the mantle to Robin. In those texts, though, Batman doesn't end: Miller wrote a sequel called *The Dark Knight Strikes Back*, and Morrison only trapped Bruce Wayne in the past, where he can eventually be rescued and resume his Batman identity. Actually ending, and definitively ending, a comic-book myth is not as easy as it looks.

This is why Gaiman's *Caped Crusader* is so important and so brilliant. Whether or not you find the solution of Batman's eternal recurrence satisfying, it is a philosophically meaningful conclusion to Batman's story. By giving us a resolution where Bruce Wayne ends his life by beginning to relive his life again, Gaiman allows no external reward or justification for Batman's existence. Any significance in Batman's life lies not in some *telos*, destination, or final victory, but rather in the life itself. Gaiman transforms Batman into the ultimate Nietzschean figure, one who celebrates life by repeating life.

Superman's Happily Ever After

Caped Crusader is modeled after a classic 1983 Superman comic, *Whatever Happened to the Man of Tomorrow?* For that comic, DC editors challenged Alan Moore (who also wrote *Watchmen*) to imagine what the very last issues of *Superman* would look like. Moore gave us a rousing and now classic take on Superman. Superman's greatest enemies team up, with Lex Luthor and Brainiac getting fused into one. They lay siege to the Fortress of Solitude, and Superman fights a desperate and losing battle against them. In the end, he can only triumph by giving up his superpowers and faking his own death. While this may seem tragic—Superman without powers!—this ending allows Superman to become a "normal" person. While the world thinks Superman's dead, he has actually retired, and is living in domestic bliss with Lois Lane and their young, superpowered son.

Moore, known for being a radical and ornery author (and for his wild beard[2]), is very conventional here. Superman gets to live happily ever after with the woman of his dreams, and in the end, he gets his reward. It's a nice *telos*, and a comforting end to Superman. But Superman is a far sunnier figure than Batman, and Moore's happy ending to Superman only makes Gaiman's strange ending to Batman stand out all the more.

Batman's Eternally Ever After

Caped Crusader begins with Batman realizing that he has just died. Led by a mysterious spirit guide, he attends his own funeral. All of Batman's greatest friends and enemies show up, and they proceed to tell stories about Batman's death. The reader quickly realizes that all of these stories contradict each other, and that this isn't a normal ghostly funeral, but rather some multi-dimensional mish-mash that's not going to provide the "true" story of Batman's death. After listening to several stories, Batman's spirit guide reveals that she is Batman's mother, and she tells Batman that his ultimate fate is to be reborn as the infant Bruce Wayne, to be Batman all over again.

The confusing, contradictory stories of Batman's death work to prepare readers for Gaiman's move to eternal recurrence. The content of these stories calls into question the deepest supposed meanings of Batman's war on crime. Having painted himself into a corner with a narrative that questions the very meaning of Batman's existence, Gaiman extricates himself with a turn to eternal recurrence.

Let's start by looking at the specific problems *Caped Crusader* raises. You don't need a solution as bizarre (and powerful) as eternal recurrence without some serious crises. Many of these are the basic questions of the Batman story: What does Batman's life mean? Does his war on crime have any greater significance? Any resolution? What kind of reward would such a life call for? The first portions of *Caped Crusader* work to eliminate any conventional answers to these questions, and only then can Gaiman introduce the idea of eternal recurrence.

Gaiman starts his narrative ordinarily enough, with Detective Gordon summarizing Batman's fate: "That one day

---

[2] Seriously, google his picture.

someone would say, 'Hey, Jim. Whatever happened to the Caped Crusader?' I'd tell them, 'pretty much what you'd expect. He's dead.' I just didn't think it would be today" (*Batman: Whatever Happened to the Caped Crusader?*). From that conventional beginning, you might expect the volume to explain how Batman died, but Gaiman undermines the expectations of his audience. As we read the stories of Batman's death, we gradually realize that none of them is the "definitive" story. Instead, we can read them as stories of alternative realities, stories of other Batmans on other Earths (a common comic-book device), all leading eventually to the same conclusion: one dead Batman. It is the content of these stories, though, that undermines any conventional ending to the Batman saga.

"The Cat-Woman's Tale" is about the strained romance between Batman and Catwoman. Narrated by Catwoman, this story focuses on the possibility that Catwoman and Batman might eventually become a couple. Early in the story, Catwoman goes so far as to almost propose marriage to Batman: "You could stop. We could be normal together."

Batman refuses.

Later, he's badly wounded while out fighting crime. He limps to Catwoman's cat store and asks for help. Instead of helping him, Catwoman simply ties him up and lets him to bleed to death. The lesson: don't spurn Catwoman. More than that, though, "The Cat-woman's Tale" is Gaiman's direct response to the domestic bliss found in *Whatever Happened to the Man of Tomorrow?* By showing Batman's greatest love interest killing him, Gaiman tells his audience that there can be no happily ever after for Batman, no cozy household with little BatCat-children running around.

So the first story removes one possible ending, and Gaiman's second tale further undermines the "truth" of the Batman mythos. In "The Gentleman's Gentleman's Tale," Alfred, Batman's longtime butler, admits that he was the man behind everything. Alfred reveals that he was once an actor, and that, after Bruce's parents died, he hired some of his former colleagues to "intrigue Master Bruce" by pretending to be "master criminals." By giving Bruce something to do, these play criminals would help Batman "when the black mood came upon him." This works for a while, but eventually Batman needs a

"Moby Dick for his Ahab," so Alfred dresses up as a character called the Joker, and "those were the glory days."

Bruce Wayne eventually uncovers the deception, and realizes that "it's all been a lie? Everything I've done? All a lie?" Alfred answers that, "Not at all, sir. If you believed that you were fighting evil, then you were indeed fighting evil." Few readers will accept such a twisted bit of logic: if the Joker wasn't real, what does Batman's war on crime mean? Alfred's story removes any transcendent or ultimate meaning to Batman's existence. By giving us this alternative version, without any real criminals, Gaiman forces us to re-examine some of the most cherished values of that myth and to question whether the Batman story has any legitimacy or meaning.

Caped Crusader plunges the reader (and Batman) into a world without ultimate meaning. Batman himself is shown to have no stable, fixed personality. Domestic bliss is taken off the table, and the very identity of his most cherished villains, such as the Joker, is subject to change. Since Batman encounters all of this as his soul is in transit to some sort of afterlife, the lack of stability—rather than an emergence of it—deeply undermines the concept of a tidy teleological ending for Batman. Without a *telos*, the audience is ready for eternal recurrence.

Batman Without End

Gaiman crystallizes the affirming nature of eternal recurrence during *Caped Crusader's* conclusion. As the volume concludes, we hear that, "It doesn't matter what the story is, some things never change." Eventually, the spirit guide reveals herself as Bruce's mother, and she says to Bruce: "Do you know the only reward you get for being Batman? You get to be Batman."

His mother tells him that the cycle will begin again: "You can stop fighting now . . . just for a few more years . . . it's over." The final panels show Batman dying, and then being reborn as Bruce Wayne once again, to begin his life over, to suffer through all of the pain, the loss of his parents, becoming Batman, all his triumphs and defeats, his eventual death and rebirth.

Without the knowledge of eternal recurrence's life affirming qualities, this ending would be intensely depressing. If we return to Batman's mother's assessment, that the only reward of being Batman is to be Batman, we can see how

Gaiman utilizes the philosophical meaning of eternal recurrence. Gaiman gives us a new method for embracing the Batman mythos: instead of the problems of Batman needing some sort of exterior resolution, of victory, their repetition becomes the reward itself. This move forces us to stop looking outside the mythos for grander meaning to the Batman story (victory over evil, affirmation of domesticity or American values, or some such). The meaning of the Batman myth is the Batman myth, eternally repeated.

Through eternal recurrence, Gaiman is able to reveal a fundamental truth about us and Batman. We never want Batman to end. We want him to be Batman forever, to continue fighting the Joker forever, and to have no meaning except in being Batman. In many ways, Gaiman's turn to eternal recurrence is one of the most fitting possible conclusions to the Batman mythos. Instead of forcing readers to look outside of that story for resolution, to some other value system, it identifies the reward of Batman as Batman itself.

One of the more fascinating aspects of *Caped Crusader* is how Gaiman is able to deliver a vision of Batman's ending that is both consistent with the Batman universe and with Gaiman's own literary interests. This idea of repetition is drawn from the very structure of the Batman myth, since Batman is already repeating himself endlessly throughout thousands of comics, movies, and television shows. What Gaiman has done is to take one of the fundamental traits of the comic—its recursive quality—and spun a philosophical meaning from that. In the comics, Batman is doomed to live the same life over and over again. After all, he's a fictional character. He's was fighting the Joker fifty years ago, and he'll be fighting the Joker fifty years from now. If you try to find the meaning of Batman's life outside of the idea of Batman, you'll fail. Gaiman shows us that only by valuing the very repetition of Batman can we embrace Batman himself.

Gaiman Endlessly Repeating

Once you've seen how eternal recurrence works in *Caped Crusader*, it's easy to look back over Gaiman's other works and find similar repetitions elsewhere. Many, if not all, of Gaiman's characters are caught up in cycles of recurrence, preventing them from reaching any final ending. Take *American Gods*: "'Not only are there no happy endings,' she told him, 'there aren't even any endings'" (p. 483). We could use that line as the slogan for *Caped Crusader*.

Not all of Gaiman's repetitions and recurrences fit neatly into the Nietzschean mold. This is a good thing, of course. We wouldn't want Gaiman to be so predictable. Instead, Gaiman plays with the ideas of eternity and repetition throughout his works. By doing so, Gaiman is asking—indeed, forcing—his readers to think of existence not in relationship to a fixed end point, but rather in relationship to the lived experience itself.

The seemingly dramatic "ending" of *The Sandman* series is an excellent example of this. Gaiman follows the death of Morpheus (Dream) in *The Sandman: The Kindly Ones* with the emergence of a new Dream. In *The Sandman: The Wake*, Gaiman shows various characters from *The Sandman* universe struggling to make sense of Dream's death. As one incarnation of Sandman dies, another comes to be, and yet as, the new Dream puts it, "I have existed since the beginning of time. This is a true thing. I am older than worlds and suns and gods. But tomorrow I will meet my brothers and sisters for the first time. And I am afraid" (*The Sandman: The Wake*, p. 49). Other characters are equally confused: has anything ended?

Dream is caught in a different cycle of repetition and recurrence than Batman. While Batman was going an exact repetition of his life, Dream is both brand new and immortal at the same time. We're out of Nietzsche's specific territory here, but still in the same general vicinity. The repetition of Dream—from one incarnation to another—forces readers to ask the same questions about Dream as we asked about Batman. Since there is no "eternity" or "reward" for Dream after his existence, how are we to value his life? While *The Wake* does not feature recurrence in the exact same way as *Caped Crusader*, there are clear similarities across the volumes. Gaiman has even gone so far as to repeat aspects of *The Wake* in *Caped Crusader*, as both use the funeral as a central motif for concluding a comic-book series.

We could keep going and find all sorts of other cycles, repetitions, and recurrences in Gaiman's fictional universes. While these are not all close to Nietzschean eternal recurrence, together they show how haunted Gaiman is by Nietzsche's myth.

13
Four Bikers of the Apocalypse

TUOMAS W. MANNINEN

Fictional characters and fictional objects present a bit of a problem to philosophers. What's the problem? Put simply, they don't exist.

Plato already noted the problem in his *Sophist*: if something doesn't exist, then how can we even talk about it? (*Sophist*, line 237e). What makes matters even worse is that we want to make *true* claims about fictional characters. We want to say that the statement, "Aziraphale is a proprietor of a used book store who has an extensive collection of rare prophetic texts" is true, and that "Aziraphale is a bar owner" is false.

This seems to make sense. In a way, these claims compare favorably to claims like "Neil Gaiman is a popular British-born novelist" (true) and "Neil Gaiman is the head coach of the US national field hockey team, who loathes black T-shirts, and doesn't think that comics are a respectable art" (false, on all three counts).

But the claims about Neil Gaiman are made true by facts about the person Neil Gaiman. What makes the claims about Aziraphale true, if Aziraphale does not exist? According to the correspondence theory of truth, a claim is true if and only if it accurately represents the world, and false otherwise. But try as we might to search the world, we can't find an entity that corresponds to Aziraphale. Or Crowley. Or London Below. Or . . . you get the picture; none of these fictional entities exist in the real world, unlike their author, who does.

Let's brush that problem aside. Whether you like it or not—and a lot of philosophers don't—I'm going to assume (as most readers of fiction do) that fictional objects do exist, even if not in the same way that their authors do. Having made this assumption, we now run into a further problem.

A common feature in Neil Gaiman's writing is his use of mythological figures as characters. We have Morpheus, the god of dreams as the title character in the *Sandman* comics; in *American Gods*, we have a plethora of deities; in *Anansi Boys*, we have the spider god; and *Good Omens* features the Four Horsemen—or, horsepersons—of the Apocalypse. All these characters have their origins elsewhere, either in oral tradition or with some other author. So what's the problem here? The trouble is that Gaiman's use of the characters goes against the original authors' description of the characters.

A Puzzle and a Solution

If we were dealing with just one author, we could say that using the same character with different descriptions is just something the author's entitled to do. It's just a matter of character development. If the author who has written about a character (like Gaiman who wrote about the two angels Crowley and Aziraphale in *Good Omens*) subsequently pens another story featuring these characters, it poses no difficulties to suppose that these are the same fictional characters. For example, Neil Gaiman and Terry Pratchett wrote a short story, "Crowley and Aziraphale's New Year's Resolutions," featuring the two angels from *Good Omens*. Two authors here, Neil Gaiman and Terry Pratchett, but it's the same duo who wrote both pieces. So here there seems to be no problem.

But Gaiman's approach to mythology goes beyond this. After all, he wasn't the original author of the myths on which *Sandman* is based. Or, for that matter, the original author of the stories where the cast of *American Gods* are first found. We could argue that Gaiman takes the character of, say, Odin in Norse myths and bases his character of Mr. Wednesday on those. Granted, Mr. Wednesday has characteristics that cannot be found in the older descriptions of Odin. But this just follows from the fact that any literary description of a character is incomplete. Gaiman completes the description in a way that remains true to the original descriptions. Mr. Wednesday is just Odin situated in a new environment.

This may solve one problem, but another one remains: what is the nature of this historical constraint? And could Gaiman revise the character in a way to make it better suited to his story? This problem is aggravated in *Good Omens*, especially in the case of the Four Riders of the Apocalypse.

When John of Patmos wrote *The Revelation of Jesus Christ*, the Second Horseman, War, is described as follows: War rides a red horse,

> and power was given to him that sat thereon to take peace from the earth, and that they should kill one another: and there was given unto him a great sword. (*Revelation* 6:4, in the King James Translation)

In *Good Omens*, Gaiman's description of War is vastly different.[1] She (not he) is known as Scarlett, who has made a killing—excuse the pun—by selling arms to various (and typically, all) sides of conflicts worldwide; later (after getting bored of her profession) she is known as Carmine "Red" Zuigiber, the most successful war correspondent there was, who has an uncanny talent of going where wars will be. She still wears red, and she still rides red—a red motorcycle as a Hell's Angel (one of the original four, representing the chapter of "Revelations 6").

On the face of it, the characters depicted in these two works seem to be worlds apart from one another. These two accounts are inconsistent with one another: the properties ascribed to War in *Revelation* and the properties ascribed to her in *Good Omens* are such that they cannot be borne by one and the same entity. Because War was described as a man, it would be false to say that he is not a man, on the pain of logical contradiction (at least, absent a sex-change operation). The approach we considered—that Gaiman (or any author, for that matter) merely develops the character from the work of another author— seems to run into limitations here. In violating the historical constraint, Gaiman seems to have introduced a wholly new character, which bears some resemblance to the original character from Revelation.

----

[1] I'm following Pratchett—who gives most of the credit to Gaiman—in referring to Gaiman as the sole author of these characters. For Pratchett's interview, see <http://www.lspace.org/books/apf/words-from-the-master.html>.

And what about the other three of the four? Famine—or Dr. Raven Sable—seems to have undergone a similar character transformation. In a way, Famine still measures wheat and barley; he just keeps them out from of diet plan advanced by his global corporation, Newtrition. The methods of the Famine of *Revelation* and Dr. Sable of *Good Omens* may have changed, but the end results are much the same: by following the diet plan he advocates, "It didn't matter how much you ate, you lost weight. And hair. And skin tone. And, if you ate enough of it long enough, vital signs" (*Good Omens*, p. 138).

Two down. The next one—Pestilence—seems to be a different matter. As it turns out, he retired from the group in 1936 ("muttering something about penicillin") and was replaced by Gaiman's character, Pollution. The fourth and final horseman, Death, seems to be the only traditionalist in the group. While the other three have kept up with the times, Death has not had the leisure to do so. And being a true professional, he's carried on his craft while others have explored alternate career paths.

The matters get further complicated if we turn to Gaiman's other works, like *Sandman*. And they become even more so if we consider his co-author's (Pratchett's) works. Death, as he appears in *Good Omens* bears a striking resemblance to Death in Pratchett's *Discworld*: both are tall, gaunt, scythe-wielding skeletons that TALK LIKE THIS. But neither of these two Deaths comes close to Death as she appears in Gaiman's *Sandman*: a charming, affable, young goth woman who prefers casual clothes over the more traditional black robes, but who still acts as a psychopomp for the departed souls.

The problem with the theory that authors simply develop the characters that originate in other authors' works is that it cannot really be applied across the board. First, it is rather limited, in that it allows only the unmentioned features of fictional characters to be addressed. Second, if we want to make changes to the characters—as Gaiman is wont to do—we're forced to make *ad hoc* modifications if we want to say that the Four Horsemen of *Revelation* and the Four Horse—well, persons—of *Good Omens* are the same characters.

But why should we accept the historical constraint? The philosopher David Lewis maintained in his classic paper "Truth in Fiction" that when we want to make truthful claims about fictional characters, the original author's word is the ultimate arbiter on the characteristics of a character. Although this seems to leave room for some of Gaiman's revisionary mythology (developing the characters in a way that doesn't conflict with the original description), it restricts the author's hand quite a bit in some ways. Also, Lewis's theory doesn't tell us much about fictional characters. We get true statements such as "In the book *Good Omens*, the angel Aziraphale is a proprietor of a used book store," but what about statements such as "Aziraphale is a character created by Neil Gaiman," or "Neil Gaiman's character War is based on the character in *Revelation*"?

Lewis's theory helps us when we're making claims in the context of fiction, or in the context of real life. But what about statements that combine real-life, actual individuals with fictional ones? Gaiman frequently does this, by supplying historical individuals with fictional narratives. Take Elvis Presley and the unnamed cook at Burger Lord in Des Moines, Iowa, in *Good Omens*. Or take Joshua Abraham Norton, the self-proclaimed Emperor of America, or Maximilien Robespierre, a key figure in the French Revolution as they appear in "Fables and Reflections" (*Sandman* #31 "Thermidor," and #29 "Three Septembers and a January," respectively). Here Gaiman didn't entirely invent the characters, but only augmented reality with his creative license.

So what are we talking about when we talk about these characters? Are we talking about nothing at all? Can we do better?

A Better Solution?

Yes, we can. We started with the assumption that fictional characters exist. But just as we acknowledge this, at the same time we want to say that they don't exist—at least not in the same way as you exist, or I exist, or Neil Gaiman exists. So what are they? I don't mean what are They? I mean what are they? "They," as we all know, are the group of friends—Pepper, Wensleydale, and Brian—led by Adam Young, the Antichrist, in *Good Omens*; "they" refers to fictional characters in general.

One answer is that fictional characters are abstract artifacts created by their authors; this view is proposed by Amie Thomasson in her book *Fiction and Metaphysics*. Artifacts are objects that have been created with some intention in mind. Artifacts, whether they're concrete or abstract, are dependent on their creators (sometimes individuals, sometimes a whole group of them): they would not exist if some being had not intended to make an object of that particular kind.

If fictional characters are abstract artifacts, this means that they are artifacts without any physical location in space and time. The book or e-book reader that you're holding is a concrete artifact. So is the laptop computer I used to write this chapter. In contrast, fictional entities—whether characters like Aziraphale and Crowley, things like *Nice and Accurate Prophecies of Agnes Nutter*, the brass scales received by Dr. Sable, or places like Lower Tadfield—don't have a physical location in space and time.

Granted, there are some similarities—the world occupied by all the above also contains places called London and Des Moines, Iowa. But these are just the abstract counterparts of the actual places. An advantage of the artifact theory is that it captures a crucial point about fictional objects including fictional characters—that they are created by their respective authors.

When Gaiman wrote *Sandman*, he created the artifact "Death." Other authors have used a similar character in their stories—Terry Pratchett's "Death" first appeared in *The Colour of Magic*; Ingmar Bergman used "Death" as one of the characters in *The Seventh Seal*, and so on. But Pratchett had created a different artifact called "Death," and likewise for Bergman (and for all the authors): each of these is a different and separate artifact from Gaiman's. This much is similar for other artifacts: the computer I have used to write this essay is not the same computer as you (the reader) have at your desk—even though both are computers, and may even be of the same model.

So now we have a theory of what fictional objects are. How does this theory help us with our particular problem? When John of Patmos, the author of *Revelation*, created War (and the other Horsemen), he ascribed to them some specific features. This goes quite nicely along with Amie Thomasson's analysis: John of Patmos's creative work (whether abetted by ingesting "odd mushrooms" or not is beside the point) brought to existence the abstract entities we collectively know as the Four Horsemen. And due to his creative choices we can make truthful claims about them. But when Gaiman goes and changes the properties (of the character War, or any other character, for that matter) considerably, is he modifying the original artifact?

Again, it seems that we haven't escaped the original problem: the constraints posed by the original creative act still remain. How can we make any modifications to the fictional characters? The easy solution would be to say that this is not possible. John of Patmos created the abstract artifacts known as the Four Horsemen of the Apocalypse, and Neil Gaiman created another set of abstract artifacts known as the Four Riders of the Apocalypse. The two sets of entities are not identical to one another, so the problem goes away.

Yet this isn't an entirely satisfactory answer, especially given Gaiman's story-telling technique. We still want to say that the Four Riders of the Apocalypse are related to the Four Horsemen of the Apocalypse. And if we take a closer look at artifacts, we can have our cake and eat it too. To do this, we need to start from the original artifacts created by John of Patmos. When he created the Four Horsemen, what exactly did he create? A short answer is that he created both an artifact type and artifact tokens.

Consider the word "artifact." If I were to ask you *how many letters are there in the word "artifact?"*, you could answer "Eight." Alternatively, you could have answered "Six." Both answers would be correct. The first answer counted all the individual letters—or each letter *token*. The second answer counted all the different letter *types*; since "a" and "t" each appear twice, the word contains six different letter types. When it comes to objects in the world, we can have multiple instances (tokens) of the same type. There are thousands of tokens of the book *Neil Gaiman and Philosophy*, yet all the tokens are of the same type.

The Four Horsemen created by John of Patmos and the Four Bikers created by Gaiman are different *tokens* of the *type* that was also created by John of Patmos. Something very similar can be readily witnessed with other artifacts; a prototype can be developed in many and various ways, and each of the tokens can still be seen as an instance of the artifact type. Likewise, when an author takes a character developed by another author, they create another token of the original type. This raises the question, to what extent can the artifact type be modified and yet remain of that type?

Aziraphale's Bible collection is quite a nice illustration of this point. The Wicked Bible, for instance, is a copy of the King James Bible—but not an identical one. The omission of a single "not" in the seventh commandment (in *Exodus* 20:14), due to a mistake in the typesetting, is the source for why the Wicked Bible is of a different type than the King James Bible. We can take a more concrete example to illustrate this point—a knife, say. The earliest knives were artifacts all right, as were all the subsequent ones. But consider the development of knives from the early flint knives through the Bronze Age, Iron Age, and onto the Industrial Age: there are marked differences in the materials used. The function, however, remains much the same. Sure, there are more specialized knives—those that are for cutting, those that are for stabbing, those that are for ornamental purposes, and so on. But they still fall under the general concept of "knife."

The Same Character . . . ?

According to the artifact theory of fiction, fictional characters are abstract artifacts created by their authors. Once we draw the distinction between artifact types and artifact tokens, we find that the same type can have many individual tokens falling under it. But this now seems to call for another restriction: doesn't there have to be something in common to all of the individual tokens of the type? For if there isn't, why would they be tokens of that type?

What features must all artifacts of the type "War" have in common? Do they all need to be called by the same name? That criterion would exclude Carmine "Red" Zuidberg from the list; likewise, Mr. Wednesday would not be Odin. And on the flip side, consider Door (from *Neverwhere*): by this reasoning, we would have to include a lot of structural objects from the local hardware store among that type. What about appearance? Again, too bad for Red (and too bad for Death in *Sandman*). This criterion seems just too restrictive. Just a brief attempt at finding the criteria by which all and only the tokens of a type are tokens of that type leads us to problems. We miss the mark, either by bringing in too many unrelated entities, or by leaving out some related entities.

Luckily, there's a way around this problem. The philosopher Ludwig Wittgenstein pointed out that if we use the same word for a lot of different things, it doesn't follow that all of them have some one quality or characteristic in common. Wittgenstein illustrated this with the concept of games, and maintained that not all games have one thing in common. Instead, there are a lot of overlapping similarities covering some but not all types of games, what Wittgenstein called 'family resemblances'.

This is a bit like the similarities we see in a collection of family members, such as the family lineage that goes from Agnes Nutter to her son John Device, ultimately reaching Anathema Device through all the generations in between. We would not find just one feature (or one set of features) that all and only the members of that family have. Instead, we would find a lot of overlapping similarities, "a complicated network of similarities overlapping and criss-crossing: sometimes overall similarities, sometimes similarities of detail" (Wittgenstein, *Philosophical Investigations*, §66). So this gives us a handle on the problem: we can classify all the different tokens of a type of fictional object, such as the rider Death, as one character, because all the different versions are united by a family resemblance,.

Artifacts are created. For concrete artifacts, this doesn't seem to be a problem. Here we have the concrete product that depends on its author's creative acts. But how can we create abstract artifacts? Aren't we just making s#@! up? This act of creating nonexistent objects seems awfully like the powers wielded by Fat Charlie Nancy's father: making things happen just by saying it. But on a close inspection, we see that this is not such an uncanny power after all. There are quite a few cases when we do things with words. When a minister proclaims to a couple "I now pronounce you husband and wife" he's not merely describing a fact. Instead, he's making that fact true by saying those words. He's performing a linguistic act that changes reality. This happens only in specific contexts—most often, saying that something is so doesn't make it so. But there are cases where it does. Authors like Gaiman creating fictional characters is just a parallel case to this: under the right circumstances, they can bring abstract entities into existence.

What Might Be

We've arrive at one answer to the philosophical question raised by Gaiman's invention of fictional characters. But it's by no means the only one.

After returning to London Above in *Neverwhere*, Richard Mayhew experiences, shall we say, difficulties in adjusting back to life in the real world. On a night out with his soon-to-be-former-friends, he explains to Gary (from Corporate Accounts) that he hadn't—not really—been to Majorca. Ultimately, Richard decides to return to London Below. For him, the ordinary life—the life he's always wanted—has turned out not to be true after all. Or it was true only in a very limited sense.

The exchange between Richard and Gary could just as well have been had by the philosopher Bertrand Russell and someone Russell (in *The Problems of Philosophy*) dubs "a practical man": a person who assesses the worth of philosophy by its practical consequences. Basically, Russell defends philosophy as valuable (or, more precisely, invaluable) even though it hardly provides these practical consequences. Rather, philosophy provides answers to questions that fall beyond the scope of specialized sciences, but its answers may not be demonstrably true.

At the end of *Neverwhere*, Richard Mayhew opts to return to London Below. Gary takes a taxi back home, ostensibly worried about Richard's well-being (not to mention sanity). Richard's description of what he has experienced has not convinced Gary, even if Richard himself is willing to return to London Below. The same can frequently happen in philosophy. A philosophical answer may fail to convince you, but this doesn't mean that nothing has been gained. As Russell put the point, "while diminishing our feeling of certainty as to what things are," philosophy "greatly increases our knowledge as to what they may be" (*Problems of Philosophy*, p. 157). So I make no claim that this is the final word—that this is *how it has to be* when it comes to fictional objects. But this is how it could be.

14
Nobody's Home

ROBERT T. TALLY JR.

The climactic moment of Neil Gaiman's *The Graveyard Book* is not a fierce duel between the forces of good and evil, a thrilling escape from the jaws of death, the solution to an enigmatic mystery, or a discovery of some long-lost treasure (although it is also all of these), but a simple statement, calmly spoken by the hero.

> Bod felt the cold of the knife at his neck. And in that moment, Bod understood. Everything slowed. Everything came into focus. "I know my name," he said. "I'm Nobody Owens. That's who I am." (*The Graveyard Book*, p. 282)

A living child who is raised by cemetery ghosts and the undead, Bod is able to exist in the space between worlds. Gaiman's novels frequently explore this shimmering realm of the "in-between": between the worlds of myth and reality (as in *American Gods* and *Anansi Boys*), between alternate universes through the looking-glass (*Neverwhere*, *Coraline*, or *Stardust*), between the mundane and the otherworldly (*Good Omens*), or between the realms of the living and of the dead (here in *The Graveyard Book*). Often, this in-between space defines the horizon of being for the principal characters, who must actively engage in an exploration of their own sense of self. In many of Gaiman's novels the hero's journey is one of self-discovery, while also being a quest of *self-making*. In the case of Nobody Owens, the self-making project involves coming to terms with the ghostly world of the living as well as of the dead.

This spectral philosophy calls to mind the existentialist thought of Jean-Paul Sartre and of Martin Heidegger, while also adding the profound effects of the otherworldly. In Sartre, for instance, the imperative to live authentically, to understand one's project in life, and to affirm one's place in the world, underscores the very meaning of existence, meaning which is created by the individual subject itself. But this is occasioned by anxiety, a sense of the uncanny or of not-being-at-home with the situation one finds oneself in.

In *The Graveyard Book*, however, Nobody's *home* lies directly in this space between worlds, as his freedom includes "the Freedom of the Graveyard" (p. 38) and his experience in this spectral, in-between zone makes his existence all the more exemplary. If the project of our existence is to make ourselves "at home" in the world, then the tale of Nobody Owens offers a marvelously apt portrait of how to live well, by coming to terms with our place in the world of the living, the dead, and those that lie in between.

Nobody but Himself

The Graveyeard Book opens with one of the most frightening scenes in all of Gaiman's works, as a murderous "man Jack," wielding a razor-sharp knife and having already killed two adults and one child, methodically stalks his final victim, an unnamed baby who by chance manages to elude his pursuer by toddling up to a nearby cemetery. The infant is discovered and taken in by the ghosts of the graveyard, who are entreated to save the baby from the killer by a new, shrieking ghost (the just-murdered mother of the baby). The novel thus begins, literally, in the shadow of death, and emphasizes the fragility of existence from the start. Thrust into this precarious life, the boy called Nobody will have to make sense of his Being in the face of the nothingness confronting it at all times. In Sartre's estimation, so do we all.

In having its ghosts decide the fate of the boy, *The Graveyard Book* also begins to establish its existential themes. Those *who are no longer* take responsibility for *the one who is*, and this boy's identity is established at the getgo by his being *himself*. For example, when the ghosts are arguing over what to name the foundling, each suggesting the names of persons he looks like, his adoptive mother (Mrs. Owens) interjects: "He looks like nobody but himself. . . . He looks like nobody." Silas, the mysterious figure who becomes the boy's guardian, settles it. "'Then Nobody it is,' said Silas. 'Nobody Owens.'" Asked what kind of name that is for a boy, Silas responds: "His name. And a good name" (p. 25).

The naming of Nobody, combined with the adoption by the Owenses, provide the hero with a name that directly links his personal existence to its own unique condition. Who he is *is* who he is. Or, to put it another way, Nobody is himself unlike all others—"he looks like nobody but himself"—and his independence is underscored by his name, echoing the nursery rhyme Gaiman uses for the novel's epigraph: "It's only a pauper / Who nobody owns." The naming of Nobody Owens thus establishes the principal existential theme of the entire novel: your essence lies in your own existence.

Although existentialism is not really a formal school of thought with easily agreed-upon principles and established methods, we can identify a few recognizable features that characterize existentialism as a philosophy. The foundational observation by Sartre is that "Existence precedes essence," a slogan derived from a phrase in Heidegger's *Being and Time*, "The 'essence' of Dasein lies in its existence" (*Being and Time*, p. 67). *Dasein*, a term that could be literally translated as "being-there" (but which is usually left untranslated), is Heidegger's term for what we might just call individual existence in a common-sense way—a person actually living in the world. Hence, what Heidegger means is that the fundamental or essential aspect of being-in-the-world, of actually existing people, is *that* they exist. Nothing more, and certainly nothing less either.

There is no pre-existent essence (a soul, for example, that exists before we are born) of which existence is a mere secondary form or manifestation. Referring to this as the "first principle of existentialism," Sartre explains:

> What do we mean here by "existence precedes essence"? We mean that man first exists: he materializes in the world, encounters himself, and only afterwards defines himself. If man as existentialists conceive of him cannot be defined, it is because to begin with he is nothing. He will not be anything until later, and then he will be what he makes of himself. (*Existentialism Is a Humanism*, p. 22)

For Sartre, it follows that, with no inherent human nature, no eternal or transcendent purpose with which to justify our existence—that is, no prior "meaning of life"—we must create our own meaning. With no inherent meaning to our existence, no essential being other than the *existing* being, we cannot look outside of actually existing reality for answers to the question of the meaning of life, and so on. Moreover, human beings are situated in the world and cannot stand outside of it, so all actions necessarily take place in relation to an actually existing world, without reference to an otherworldly ideal.

Gaiman's spectral existentialism complicates this a bit, as the real world in which we exist is fundamentally tied to an otherworldly realm, which is nevertheless also a real plane of existence. In *The Graveyard Book*, this otherworldly world includes that of the dead, but also a threshold space between the realms of the living and the dead, a space occupied by Nobody Owens, as well as several other characters in the novel.

In the graveyard, Nobody is free to choose his own path, but that path also leads him into encounters with specters. In evading the murderer in *The Graveyard Book*'s first chapter, Bod assures his continued existence by making a home of the cemetery, by living among the dead. What's more, throughout the course of the novel, Nobody is emphatically a person who forms himself, via his interactions with others—be they living, dead, or other—such as the Owenses, Silas, Scarlett, Miss Lupescu, the ghouls, the witch Liza Hempstock, his schoolmates, the Jacks, and the Sleer. Whatever identity he had prior to coming to the graveyard is simply not relevant. Indeed, we never learn exactly who the child had been before the night he came to the graveyard. Rather, we're to understand that *who Bod is* will be determined largely *by Bod* in the course of his ongoing education in the spectral realm between the living and the dead. Bod "will be what he makes of himself."

Fear and Trembling

A basic consequence of the existentialist philosophy is that a person, who embodies no essential human nature and whose life has no essential or transcendent meaning, must have the freedom to create his own meaning. This is not exactly a process of self-*discovery*, which would assume an essence out there to be discovered, but a matter of self-*fashioning*.

Who else could do it for you? In Sartrean existentialism, there is no Divine Plan or Supreme Being who can justify your existence for you, so you must have the freedom to do it yourself. And, even in those variations of existentialism that allow for a God, such as Søren Kierkegaard's Christian philosophy, man remains free to act—owing to the God-given gift of freewill (or the curse of freewill, depending on how you look at it). Kierkegaard's *Fear and Trembling* is a meditation on the fearsome "leap of faith" required by Abraham in his decision to sacrifice his son Isaac in the Book of Genesis.

Such freedom is not necessarily a blessing, and it is primarily experienced as a generalized mood of anxiety. We can understand this in the everyday sense, as when we have to make a tough decision and understandably feel anxious about it, knowing that by choosing one path we are foreclosing the possibilities offered by other paths. In existentialism, this anxiety—*Angst* in German, though the word has entered English in this existentialist sense—becomes a condition of our lives, as we are always aware of this terrible freedom to make bad choices. In Sartre's assessment, the anxiety or anguish one feels derives from the fact that "Man is condemned to be free: condemned, because he did not create himself, yet nonetheless free, because once cast into the world, he is responsible for everything he does" (*Existentialism*, p. 29). Indeed, Sartre dramatized this anxiety as *nausea*, in his novel of that name, and being nauseated is certainly not a good feeling, as Bod discovers in the company of the ghouls.

In *The Graveyard Book*, Bod's freedom is emphasized over his anxieties, partly because his "Freedom of the Graveyard," along with his training in such spectral arts as Fading or Dream-walking, enable him to make more of his project in the world (as Sartre might call it) than others. As noted below, Nobody is "at home" in the graveyard, which is literally true in the story but which also suggests a level of comfort with the very phenomenon—death—that so many other humans are anxious about. Whereas others might find their experience *uncanny*, Bod is much more comfortable, and much more able to assert himself. Here's an example of Gaiman's spectral existentialism functioning as a better philosophy of life, ironically perhaps, because it is a philosophy so in touch with the other-worldly realms of the dead. The fear and trembling that constitutes the basic human condition can be turned, by Bod, into a useful tool or even weapon (as when he uses his ghostly gifts of fear to teach his schoolyard bullies a lesson), which in turn provides a better life, both for Bod and for those he tries to protect.

In the anxiety of not knowing whether our actions are correct, we thereby acknowledge (albeit negatively) that we must have the freedom to choose the right or wrong course of action. By feeling anxious about making a mistake, therefore, we acknowledge that we are free. Bod is not immune from this. His decisions are frequently wrong, in retrospect, and he learns from his mistakes along the way.

The Graveyard Book is the type of story in which the young protagonist moves from innocence to experience, becoming a wiser (and often sadder) person by the end. But, as we've seen, the story also ends with Nobody Owens declaring his own name, *owning* it, and then setting forth on his own adventure of life. Bod is able to transform his own existential anxiety into a greater freedom by giving himself license to be himself. Despite, or rather because of, his rather uncanny childhood experiences, he is perfectly at home in his world.

The Uncanny, or, Not at Home

The anxiety that accompanies our freedom, in existentialist theory, leads to a profound sense of alienation or of the uncanny. The German word for 'uncanny' is 'unheimlich', which literally means *un-home-ly*. As Heidegger suggests, the sense of homelessness is part of the human condition, but many thinkers have emphasized how modern life has made this anxiety worse. According to Georg Lukács, "transcendental homelessness" is the basic characteristic of life in the modern world. Without some vision of a unity of man and world (a vision that the ancient Greeks presumably held), we can no longer feel at home in the world.

Silas is perhaps the embodiment of a transcendental homelessness in *The Graveyard Book*. When Bod asks Miss Lupescu what kind of person Silas is, she replies hesitantly, "He is a solitary type" (p. 71). Earlier, Bod had said that he wanted to be like Silas: "'No,' said Silas firmly. 'You do not'" (p. 38). Although it is never stated directly in the book, we're given enough clues to figure out that Silas is a vampire, neither living or dead, operating in the worlds of both, but belonging to neither. "'It must be good,' said Silas, 'to have somewhere that you belong. Somewhere that's home'" (p. 28).

The actual sadness implicit in this remark is only clear much later, as the reader gets a better sense of Silas's own identity. Notably, during the Danse Macabre, as all the living and the dead mingle in a gloriously otherworldly ballroom, Silas is left out. As an *undead* being, he can't participate in the dance, and his melancholy and longing are revealed when Bod tells him about dancing with the Lady on the Grey, who is Gaiman's exquisite figure for Death. "'I danced with the lady, Silas!' exclaimed Bod. His guardian looked almost heartbroken then, and Bod found himself scared, like a child who had woken a sleeping panther. But all Silas said was, 'This conversation is at an end'" (p. 164). That Silas is a heroic figure, not just a wise guardian of Bod, but a leading member of the Honor Guard, those who patrol the borderlands between worlds (p. 303), makes the scene more touching. Silas has no home, not even in the graveyard, where he has "but the right of abode" (p. 38), since the graveyard is home for the dead.

Few types of places are as uncanny or un-home-ly as a graveyard. Although respect for the dead demands that cemeteries be valued, most of us would not feel at home there. Michel Foucault cites the cemetery as a perfect example of the *heterotopia*, a space that (unlike utopia) is real, but is also "different" from the other social spaces in which we live. "The cemetery is certainly a place unlike ordinary cultural spaces. It is a space that is however connected with all the sites of the city-state or society or village, etc., since each individual, each family has relatives in the cemetery. In western culture the cemetery has practically always existed" ("Of Other Spaces," p. 25). Yet, in this space the connections between the living and the dead mark it with a profound otherworldliness, making it a site of imaginary fears and wonders. In the graveyard, you're certainly not at home.

Unless you are Nobody Owens, that is. Or a ghost. As Bod tells Scarlett, who marvels at his powers and his bravery: "'This is my home,' he said. 'I can do things here,'" and again "'This is my home,' said Bod. 'I'm going to protect it'" (pp. 261,

264). The anxiety that we feel in not being at home in a given situation, the alienation and fear that comes with being lost or homeless, is all the more heightened in the heterotopia of the graveyard. Even without Bod's wielding of the power of "Fear," such persons as Nick Farthing and Mo Quilling are ill at ease in a graveyard. So are many people. Thus, for Bod to be at home there, to have homely (*heimlich*) feelings in the uncanny (*unheimlich*) places, creates a curious and powerful sense of self. As in the climax of the novel, Nobody Owens knows who he is, making him a real existentialist role model for us.

At the very end of the novel, when it's becoming more difficult for him to see ghosts and the now young-adult Bod must venture into the wider world—Bod understands that, like the rest of us, he will no longer have a home in the world, but must make his own way. After asking Silas whether he will be able to return to the graveyard, and before Silas can respond, Bod "answered his own question. 'If I come back, it will be a place, but it won't be a home any longer'."

Authenticity and Bad Faith

In the existentialist lexicon, *authenticity* names the attitude in which you act in accordance with your own self, rather than in accordance with what others similarly situated might do. In other words, am I acting as *I* would act, or am I just acting as someone in general might act? For Sartre, because there is no essence that could serve as a standard of action, there is no transcendent purpose against which to measure our own actions. But through my interactions with the world, I can distinguish how I would act as myself from how I would act as merely anyone.

Authentic behavior, then, would refer to acts done strictly as myself, observing Polonius's famous advice to Laertes in *Hamlet*: "To thine own self be true." (In *Hamlet*, Polonius appears as a self-satisfied old fart, so Shakespeare is likely making fun of this trite slogan.) A better example may come from Mrs. Owens's observation about the toddler Nobody, insofar as he is "nobody but himself," which he subsequently proves through his own words and deeds. For Sartre, authenticity requires you to act according to your true self; you must embrace your freedom to act by "owning" your acts. Be yourself, rather than being like what you think you'd be expected to be like by others. In Sartre's view, people who are inauthentic in their actions are acting in *bad faith*.

In *The Graveyard Book*, the sense of being true to yourself is made more interesting and more complex. In Chapter Three, "The Hounds of God," we are introduced to Miss Lupescu, who orders Bod to "Name the different kinds of people," to which Bod humorously guesses the living, the dead, and ". . . Cats?" (p. 70). Lupescu corrects him: "there are the living and the dead, there are day-folk and night-folk, there are ghouls and mist-walkers, there are high hunters and the Hounds of God. Also, there are solitary types" (p. 71). In enumerating the "kinds of people," Miss Lupescu might be suggesting what the "true" nature of these types is, thus establishing what kinds of actions are authentic. We learn that she is herself a lycanthrope or werewolf, who prefer to call themselves "Hounds of God" (p. 97), and who or what she is also determines how she acts. Yet, as Silas notes towards the novel's end, and as we should always remember, "People can change" (p. 303). But there are also wonderful cautionary examples in *The Graveyard Book*, and my favorite is certainly the particular "kind of person" who is the most inauthentic, whose identities and actions are merely scavenged or copied from others rather than created by and for oneself. Here we meet the very avatars of bad faith: the ghouls.

Bod meets the ghouls by their "ghoul gate," a rundown looking grave that Gaiman says exists "in every graveyard" (p. 61). The first three that Bod meets are named the honorable Archibald Fitzhugh, the Duke of Westminster, and the Bishop of Bath and Wells. By seeing these derivative names, the reader is immediately aware that ghouls have no real identity of their own, but rather leech identities from others. Just as their names are scavenged from others, so too are their lives— if such infernal creatures may be said to live—entirely inauthentic, not their own. As if to underscore the point, the ghouls tell Bod that they do not even remember who they were before they became ghouls, and despite their encouragement, this is not as comforting to Bod as they think.

> "Don't take on so," said the Duke of Westminster. "Why, you little coot, I promise you that as soon as you're one of us, you'll not ever remember as you even *had* a home."

"I don't remember anything about the days before I was a ghoul,"
said the famous writer Victor Hugo.

"Nor I," said the Emperor of China, proudly.

"Nope," said the 33rd President of the United States. (p. 86)

The ghouls are avatars of bad faith inasmuch as their entire
Being is bound up in *being-another*, as is indicated by their
derivative names. By naming one of the ghouls "the 33rd
President of the United States," Gaiman provides a small joke
that also makes this point about authenticity and bad faith, for
the 33rd US President was Harry Truman, and it can be no
accident that this inauthentic ghoul is no "true" man.

With his own very distinctive name, Nobody Owens is really
an anti-ghoul. By being himself, he distinguishes himself from
all others. Miss Lupescu gives Bod the nickname *Nimini*, which
is actually Romanian for "nobody," another of the wonderfully
understated details in Gaiman's fiction. A running gag in the
novel has Bod correcting those who would call him 'boy'. "'Bod,'
said Bod. 'It's Bod. Not boy'" (p. 67).

In his naming, Bod differentiates himself from any mere
boy; in this, Bod also registers his fundamental distinction,
rhetorically and in real life, from being merely any "man Jack."
Indeed, the real enemies in *The Graveyard Book*, somewhat
like the identity-thieving ghouls, are the almost nameless
"Jacks." To be sure, each Jack is a unique personality, but by
giving them this oh-so-common name, Gaiman makes "every
man Jack" the counterpoint to Nobody Owens. Whereas the
Jacks, like the ghouls, derive their power from other sources
and draw their magical abilities from the deaths of others (p.
270), Bod forges his own way with the aid of his friends and
family. Unlike Jack Frost, who actually revels in the deaths of
his "friends" and desires to be the Master of the Sleer, Bod recognizes that he is master of only himself—he "owns" himself
alone—and does not desire treasure or power over others. He
remains true to himself.

Self-Possession

Nobody Owens's name is itself a homonymic allusion to the epigraph of *The Graveyard Book*, a "traditional nursery rhyme"
(according to Gaiman):

Rattle his bones
Over the stones
It's only a pauper
Who nobody owns.

Although the poem's origins are not entirely clear, a famous version with these lines as the refrain is memorialized in Mary Mitford's *Recollections of a Literary Life*, where it is attributed to Thomas Noel and titled "The Pauper's Drive."

In that poem, the poet witnesses a horse-drawn hearse, speeding over the cobblestones with no regard for the solemnity of the event. The lines above are imagined as spoken by the driver, anticipating and answering the query of onlookers, effectively saying "Don't worry about the dignity of this corpse, since he's only a pauper with no family or friends." In the Noel version, several stanzas, each culminating with that refrain, describe the squalid and haphazard proceeding, before a final stanza turns the tables, as the poet himself (saddened by the events) provides his own alternative to the cab-driver's lines:

Bear softly his bones over the stones,
though a pauper, he's one whom his Maker yet owns.

In this sentimental poem, we see the wholly laudable view that each human life deserves to be treated with dignity because God, if no one else, "owns" it. But in the climactic scene of *The Graveyard Book* (in fact, at the moment of truth, which not coincidentally is also a moment of near-death), Nobody Owens claims the title of ownership of his self for himself. The Sleer has told Bod, "FIND YOUR NAME" (p. 251), and at the crucial instant, just as the vicious Jack Frost is about to tell Bod his "real" name, Bod instead "owns" the name—and moreover, the identity—he already has. "I'm Nobody Owens. That's who I am." Indeed, that's what he is. By being someone whom nobody owns, by taking ownership of his own being, Bod demonstrates his fully realized sense of self, with the freedom and self-determination that Sartre had insisted were the hallmarks of his philosophy.

During the "Danse Macabre," Bod apologetically tells the Lady on the Grey, "I don't know your name," and she responds,

"Names aren't really that important" (p. 161). And this is true, of course. Death, here figured forth as the Lady on the Grey, does not care about names, and yet the naming in *The Graveyard Book* seems so important. The mystery is easily solved in the spectral existentialism I've been discussing, however, since it is less the name itself than the self-possession, owning one's self, which is best represented by Bod's name. This then holds for one's entire life as well, as we are free to "make a name for ourselves" in our own projects in life, as when Bod sets off into the world in the final pages. As his mother, Mistress Owens, sings to him:

> Sleep my little babby-oh
> Sleep until you awaken
> When you wake you'll see the world
> If I'm not mistaken . . .
> Kiss a lover
> Dance a measure
> Find your name
> And buried treasure . . .
> Face your life
> Its pain, its pleasure,
> Leave no path untaken. (p. 306)

This is an aptly existentialist lullaby.

Learning to Live with Ghosts

Gaiman's spectral existentialism, in the end, provides a most powerful philosophy of life, a practical philosophy of *how to live*, even if this counsel frequently comes from those who are dead. The cynical might even view philosophy itself as merely taking advice from the dead—the ghosts of Plato, Spinoza, Kant, and Nietzsche—but authentic and meaningful existence, as Nobody Owens demonstrates, derives from owning oneself, which also means acknowledging the degree to which one's self is fashioned by and through those around us, including those who have come before and *are* no more.

Bod, as Jack Dandy explains it, is the prophesied "child born who would one day walk the borderland between the living and the dead" (p. 271), but the Jacks did not reckon on the fact that the reason Bod becomes that child is precisely because the Jacks tried to kill him. In this, we see the "ruse of history" (as Hegel called it) or, better, the persistence of fate. By trying to avoid the foretold outcome, you in fact become an agent of fate, helping to fulfill the prophecy.

The classic example is Oedipus, who was fated to murder his father and to wed his mother. Once his biological parents heard this prophecy, they attempted to have their newborn son killed, sending him off to be sacrificed even before naming him (like Bod, Oedipus is named by later circumstances); so Oedipus is reared by foster parents whom he believes to be his "real" parents. But, in an example of what Aristotle calls *peripeteia* or "reversal of fortune," this ensures the fulfillment of the prophecy, since Oedipus does not know his father (when he kills him) or his mother (when he marries her) *only* because he did not get to grow up with them.

The seemingly immutable destiny is also self-made. In this, Nobody Owens reminds us of our freedom to act, and encourages us to be true to ourselves by being true to our ghosts, to our family and friends, as well as acknowledging what turns out to be our wonderful *gift* of mortality. As the Lady on the Grey "promises," one day everybody gets to ride on her horse, who "is gentle enough to bear the mightiest of you away on his broad back, and strong enough for the smallest of you as well" (p. 161). Facing our own ghosts bravely and hospitably, we live our own lives better.

In Gaiman's works, life often involves juxtaposing our real world with a mirror world in which we must be made to fit with rather divergent realities—for example, a person's "self" is different in the London Below of *Neverwhere* or in the spectral "beginning of the world" in *Anansi Boys*. Hence, the existential crisis in Gaiman's novels is simultaneously compounded and disarmed, where our anxious homelessness is also a coming home or being "at home" with our self. Nobody Owens's victory comes with the climactic affirmation of his true name, which is also a no-name: "I'm Nobody Owens. That's who I am."

Gaiman's spectral existentialism provides a way of securing our sense of self that does not rely on identity or authenticity. Mother Slaughter, whose faded and weathered tombstone itself provides us with some very good advice ("LAUGH"), offers Bod even more valuable counsel at the end of *The Graveyard Book*, which we would also do well to remember: "You're always you, and that don't change, and you're always changing, and there's nothing you can do about it."

References

Arendt, Hannah. 1994 [1963]. *Eichmann in Jerusalem: A Report on the Banality of Evil*. New York: Penguin.

Aristotle. 1987. *Poetics*. Indianapolis: Hackett.

———. 1999. *Nichomachean Ethics*. Indianapolis: Hackett.

Berlant, Lauren. 1997. *The Queen of America Goes to Washington City: Essays on Sex and Citizenship*. Durham: Duke University Press.

———. ed. 2004. *Compassion: The Culture and Politics of an Emotion*. New York: Routledge.

Blum, Lawrence A. 1994. *Moral Perception and Particularity*. New York: Cambridge University Press.

Bruhm, Steven. The Contemporary Gothic: Why We Need It. In Hogle 2002.

Frances Hodgson Burnett. 1987 [1911]. *The Secret Garden*. New York: Signet.

Chalmers, David. 1996. *The Conscious Mind: In Search of a Fundamental Theory*. Oxford: Oxford University Press.

Chan, Wing-Tsit, ed. 1963. *A Sourcebook in Chinese Philosophy*. Princeton: Princeton University Press.

Chuang Tzu. The Equality of Things. In Chan 1963.

Coats, Karen. 2008. Between Horror, Humour, and Hope: Neil Gaiman and the Psychic Work of the Gothic. In Jackson, Coats, and McGilis 2008.

Cohen, Ted. 2002. Philosophy in America: Remarks on John McCumber's *Time in the Ditch: American Philosophy and the McCarthy Era*. *Philosophical Studies* 108: 1–2 (March).

Derrida, Jacques. 1994. *Specters of Marx*. London: Routledge.

———. 2001. *On Cosmopolitanism and Forgiveness*. London: Routledge.

Descartes, René. 1996. *Discourse on Method and Meditations on First Philosophy*. Binghamton: Vail-Ballou Press.

———. 1997. *Meditations on First Philosophy*. Cambridge: Cambridge University Press.

Foucault, Michel. 1977. *Discipline and Punish: The Birth of the Prison*. New York: Vintage.

———. 1986. Of Other Spaces. *Diacritics* 16.1 (Spring).

Gaiman, Neil. 1991. *The Sandman: Preludes and Nocturnes*, New York: DC Comics.

———. 1991. *The Sandman: The Doll's House*, New York: DC Comics.

———. 1992. *The Sandman: Season of Mists*. New York: DC Comics.

———. 1993. *Death: The High Cost of Living*.

———. 1996. *Neverwhere*. London: BBC.

———. 1997. *The Sandman: The Wake*. New York: DC Comics.

———. 1997. *The Day I Swapped My Dad for Two Goldfish*. Stone Mountain: White Wolf.

———. 1999. *Stardust*. New York: Morrow.

———. 2001. *American Gods*. New York: Morrow.

———. 2002. *Coraline*. New York: HarperCollins.

———. 2003. *The Wolves in the Walls*. New York: HarperCollins.

———. 2003 [1996]. *Neverwhere*. New York: HarperCollins.

———. 2005. *Anansi Boys*. New York: HarperCollins.

———. 2005. *Melinda*. New York: Hill House.

———. 2006. *Fragile Things: Short Fictions and Wonders*. New York: Morrow.

———. 2008. *The Graveyard Book*. New York: HarperCollins.

———. 2008. *Odd and the Frost Giants*. New York: HarperCollins.

———. 2008. *The Dangerous Alphabet*. New York: HarperCollins.

———. 2009. *Blueberry Girl*. New York: HarperCollins.

———. 2009. *Crazy Hair*. New York: HarperCollins.

———. 2010. *Instructions*. New York: HarperCollins.

Gaiman, Neil, Kyle Cassidy, and Beth Hommel. 2009. *Who Killed Amanda Palmer: A Collection of Photographic Evidence*. New York: Eight Foot Books.

Gaiman, Neil, and Andy Kubert. 2009. *Batman: Whatever Happened to the Caped Crusader?* New York: DC Comics. Originally published earlier the same year as *Batman* #686 and *Detective Comics* #853.

Gaiman, Neil, and Terry Pratchett. 1990. *Good Omens: The Nice and Accurate Prophecies of Agnes Nutter, Witch*. New York: Workman.

Gaiman, Neil, and Michael Reaves. 2007. *Interworld*. New York: HarperCollins.

Heidegger, Martin. 1962. *Being and Time*. New York: Harper and Row.

Herodotus. 2003. *The Histories*. New York: Penguin.

Hickman, Larry A. 2009. Why American Philosophy? Why Now? *European Journal of Pragmatism and American Philosophy*.

Hilpinen, Risto. 2011 [1999]. Artifact. *Stanford Encyclopedia of Philosophy*, <plato.stanford.edu/entries/artifact>.

Hogle, Jerrold. 2002. ed. *The Cambridge Companion to Gothic Fiction*. New York: Cambridge University Press.

Hume, David. 1988 An Abstract of *A Treatise of Human Nature*. In Hume 1988.

———. 1988 [1748]. *An Enquiry Concerning Human Understanding*. La Salle: Open Court.

———. 1992. *Writings on Religion*. La Salle: Open Court.

———. 2011 [1739]. *A Treatise of Human Nature*. Toronto: University of Toronto Libraries.

Hurley, Susan, and Stephen Shute, eds. 1994. *On Human Rights: The Oxford Amnesty Lectures 1993*. New York: Basic Books.

Jackson, Anna, Karen Coats, and Robert McGilis, eds. 2008. *The Gothic in Children's Literature: Haunting the Borders*. London: Routledge.

Jackson, Frank. 1982. Epiphenomenal Qualia. *Philosophical Quarterly* (32).

———. 1986. What Mary Didn't Know. *Journal of Philosophy* (83).

James, Henry. 1995. *The Turn of the Screw and Other Short Novels*. New York: Signet.

Kierkegaard, Søren. 2006. *Fear and Trembling*. Cambridge: Cambridge University Press.

King, Stephen. 1981. *Danse Macabre*. New York: Everest House.

Shirley Jackson, Shirley. 1959. *The Haunting of Hill House*. New York: Penguin.

Leibniz, Gottfried. 1991. *Discourse on Metaphysics and Other Essays*. Indianapolis: Hackett.

Levins-Morales, Aurora. 1998. *Medicine Stories: History, Culture and the Politics of Integrity*. Cambridge: South End Press.

Lewis, David. 1978. Truth in Fiction. *American Philosophical Quarterly* 15:1 (January).

Lukacher, Ned. 1998. *Time-Fetishes: The Secret History of Eternal Recurrence*. Durham: Duke University Press.

Lukács, Georg. 1971. *The Theory of the Novel*. Cambridge: MIT Press.

Lurie, Alison. 1990. *Don't Tell the Grown-Ups: The Subversive Power of Children's Literature*. Boston: Little, Brown.

Jean-François Lyotard. 1984 [1979]. *The Postmodern Condition*. Minneapolis: University of Minnesota Press.

May, Jill P. 1995. *Children's Literature and Critical Theory: Reading and Writing for Understanding*. New York: Oxford University Press.

Chisholm, Roderick M. 1960. *Realism and the Background of Phenomenology*. Glencoe: Free Press.

Mitford, Mary. 1883. *Recollections of a Literary Life*. London: Bentley.

Morgan, Michael L. 2008. *Discovering Levinas*. Cambridge: Cambridge University Press.

Murdoch, Iris. 2001 [1970]. *The Sovereignty of Good*. New York: Routledge.

Nagel, Thomas. 1972. What Is It Like to Be a Bat? *Philosophical Review* 83:4 (October).

Nietzsche, Friedrich. 1966. *Thus Spoke Zarathustra*. New York: Penguin.

———. 1992. *Ecce Homo*. New York: Penguin.

———. 2000. *Basic Writings of Nietzsche*. New York: Modern Library.

Katherine Paterson. 1977. *Bridge to Terabithia*. New York: HarperCollins

Penrose, Roger. 2007. *The Road to Reality: A Complete Guide to the Laws of the Universe*. New York: Vintage.

Priest, Graham. 2006. *In Contradiction: A Study of the Transconsistent*. New York: Oxford University Press.

Plato. 1963. *The Collected Dialogues*. Princeton: Princeton University Press.

Reicher, Maria. 2010 [2006]. Nonexistent Objects. *Stanford Encyclopedia of Philosophy*, <plato.stanford.edu/entries/nonexistent-objects>.

Rorty, Richard. 1993. Human Rights, Rationality, and Sentimentality. In Hurley and Shute 1993.

Rudd, David. 2008. An Eye for an I: Neil Gaiman's *Coraline* and Questions of Identity. *Children's Literature in Education* 39.

Russell, Bertrand. 1956. *Logic and Knowledge*. New York: Capricorn.

———. 1959 [1912]. *The Problems of Philosophy*. Oxford: Oxford University Press.

Sartre, Jean-Paul. 2007. *Existentialism Is a Humanism*. New Haven: Yale University Press.

Smilansky, Saul. 2007. *Ten Moral Paradoxes*. Malden: Blackwell.

Snow, Nancy E. 2005. Iris Murdoch's Notion of a Loving Gaze. *Journal of Value Inquiry* 39.

Spolsky, Ellen. 1993. *Gaps in Nature: Literary Interpretation and the Modular Mind*. Albany: State University of New York Press.

Sturluson, Snorri. 2008 [1220]. The *Prose Edda: Tales from Norse Mythology*. Mineola: Dover.

Thomasson, Amie. 1999. *Fiction and Metaphysics*. New York: Cambridge University Press.

Wittgenstein, Ludwig. 2009. *Philosophical Investigations*. Malden: Blackwell.

Behind the Scenes

NAJWA AL-TABAA is a graduate student in English Literature at the University of Florida. Her research interests include twentieth-century literature with an emphasis on American postmodern historical fiction and war, post-9/11 fiction and national trauma, science fiction and horror fiction, and comic studies. She is teaching an undergraduate class on horror fiction in the fall of 2012 and looks forward to exposing her students to the work of Neil Gaiman who is definitely on the syllabus.

TRACY L. BEALER teaches literature and composition at Metropolitan State College in Denver. She specializes in the twentieth-century American novel with a particular interest in pop culture and genre fiction. She has published on William Faulkner, Alice Walker, Quentin Tarantino, and the *Harry Potter* and *Twilight* series. She is a regular and enthusiastic attender at the biannual Whedon Studies Association *Slayage* conference, and follows Neil Gaiman's Twitter feed with a fervency bordering on pathological obsession.

JONAS-SÉBASTIEN BEAUDRY is a DPhil candidate at the University of Oxford, and regularly escapes to London Below. He worked as a Henigson Fellow (Harvard Human Rights Program) in an Argentinean human rights NGO, and served as a law clerk at the Supreme Court of Canada, and at the International Court of Justice. He also worked for the Canadian Human Rights Commission and the Inter-American Court of Human Rights. He has published scholarly articles in international law, human rights, and moral philosophy.

RAY BOSSERT is a visiting assistant professor at Franklin and Marshall College, where he teaches courses on Renaissance Literature, Shakespeare, and "Geek Lit." His academic interests range from political slave discourse in seventeenth-century England to anti-modernism in J.R.R. Tolkien. He once stood about three feet next to Neil Gaiman during the 2004 Annual Mythopoeic Conference, but could think of nothing witty to say. He would be the American God of Missed Opportunity.

BRANDON KEMPNER is an Associate Professor of English at New Mexico Highlands University. His favorite Gaiman character is Barnabas the dog, and he still holds out hope for a dog-focused *Sandman* sequel. Brandon has published articles on 9/11 fiction, on Walter Mosley and the Afrofuturist novel, on Mark Twain's influence in *Mad Men* and *The Sopranos*, and on existentialism and *The Walking Dead*.

The name GREG LITTMANN is a corruption of the Old Irish *grúac loch maccoím*, or 'hairy lake boy', a malevolent nature spirit which causes sickness in cattle if not propitiated with the sacrifice of philosophical ideas. Knowledge of the creature was brought to the Americas by Bishop Berkeley of Cloyne in the eighteenth century and Greg Littmann has since set itself up as a professor at Southern Illinois University Edwardsville, where it teaches metaphysics, epistemology, philosophy of mind, and philosophy and literature, while feasting on the thoughts of students. In deference to Apollo, Tenure, and other gods of wisdom old and new, it has published in metaphysics and the philosophy of logic and has written chapters for books relating philosophy to *Breaking Bad, Doctor Who, Dune, Final Fantasy, A Game of Thrones, The Onion*, Sherlock Holmes, and *The Walking Dead*. Greg Littmann's symbol is a textbook soaked in blood.

RACHEL LURIA has been hangin' with the Dream King since 1992, when she frequently and without remorse pillaged her friend Stephen's collection of *The Sandman* comics and wouldn't give them back until she was good and done with them. Which may or may not have been never. She is currently an assistant professor at Florida Atlantic University's Wilkes Honors College and has published numerous articles and works of fiction. Her current project is a monograph about female action heroes with co-editor Tracy Bealer.

KANDACE LYTLE is a PhD student in English at Texas Christian University in Fort Worth, and enjoys studying literature and film in relation to philosophy. When she's not doing schoolwork, Kandace is an avid writer, concert attendee, movie fanatic, and dancer who enjoys exploring liminal spaces and going on adventures with her adorable beagle Rowdy, who has no trouble passing through doors into other worlds.

TUOMAS W. MANNINEN (if you really must know) is a lecturer at the Arizona State University at the West Campus in the Division of Humanities, Arts and Cultural Studies, where he teaches many and various courses in most things philosophical. His research is focused on the metaphysics of artifacts, the metaphysics of persons, as well as on questions in philosophy of science and philosophy of religion (especially where the two fields intersect). He doesn't think too highly of daiquiris (with or without bananas), and although he doesn't expect anyone to send him money, he would *not* turn down an offer for a tenure-track position in philosophy.

WADE NEWHOUSE teaches in the English and Theatre departments at William Peace University in Raleigh. He manages to work some discussions of ghosts and haunting into almost all of his courses, which include Advanced Composition, Children's Literature, Southern Literature, and Law and Literature. He is also the Assistant Director of the improvisational comedy troupe "Raleigh's Village Idiots," and he organizes an annual improv workshop for William Peace students. Because of all this activity, Wade has been called a Jack of All Trades, but not in the immortal murdering way.

T. BRADLEY RICHARDS specializes in the philosophy of mind (the philosophy of consciousness, perception, and attention in particular). He has studied at the University of Toronto, the University of Guelph, and as a visitor to the Centre for Consciousness Studies at the Australian National University. He has written a number of screenplays, photographed bands such as Rush, and is an avid narrative and documentary filmmaker. Brad enjoys teaching philosophy, especially philosophy of film and media. He is a long-time Neil Gaiman fan.

RICHARD ROSENBAUM edits fiction for *The Incongruous Quarterly* <incongruousquarterly.com> and *Broken Pencil* magazine <broken-pencil.com>. He edited the short story anthology *Can'tLit: Fearless Fiction from Broken Pencil Magazine*. Richard has met Neil Gaiman in person twice, and one time saw him at a movie theater but didn't want to bother him.

LISA SWANSTROM is an Assistant Professor of English at Florida Atlantic University. Her areas of research include science fiction, fantasy, and the digital humanities. Before joining the English Department at FAU, she was a postdoctoral research fellow in the Digital Humanities at Umeå University's HUMlab in northern Sweden (2010), as well as the Florence Levy Kay Fellow in the Digital Humanities in the English Department at Brandeis University in Massachusetts (2008-2009). Her favorite game of chance is seven-card stud.

ROBERT T. TALLY JR. studied metaphysics and logorrhetics under Sister Mary Loquacious of the Chattering Order of St. Beryl, under whose tutelage he developed the rigorous scholarly discipline afforded by nearly uninterrupted discourse. He now teaches American and world literature at Texas State University, where he remains on the lookout for various Old World deities and the odd portal to another world. The author of *Kurt Vonnegut and the American Novel: A Postmodern Iconography* and *Melville, Mapping and Globalization: Literary Cartography in the American Baroque Writer*, Tally is also the editor of *Geocritical Explorations: Space, Place, and Mapping in Literary and Cultural Studies*.

ANDREW TERJESEN received his PhD in Philosophy from Duke University and is currently pursuing a JD at the University of Virginia School of Law. Prior to law school, he had been a visiting assistant professor of philosophy at Rhodes College, Washington and Lee University, and Austin College. Andrew has written chapters in *Sherlock Holmes and Philosophy*, *The Onion and Philosophy*, *Manga and Philosophy*, and *Supervillains and Philosophy*. Although he looks forward to becoming a lawyer, he can't imagine how Bernie Capax did it for fifteen thousand years.

WAYNE YUEN teaches philosophy at Ohlone College in Fremont. He's the editor of *The Walking Dead and Philosophy: Zombie Apocalypse Now*, as well as a contributor to *Zombies, Vampires, and Philosophy: New Life for the Undead* and *The Golden Compass and Philosophy: God Bites the Dust*. He's also pretty sure that in some kind of alternate world, be it reached by crawling through a door, using a mirror-mask, or exploring a forgotten underground, Neil Gaiman and Amanda Palmer are his super-friends where together they bring philosophy to life for the masses. Or at the very least that Neil reads him bedtime stories while Amanda sings lullabies.

Index